www.

Specialising in
wildlife developments
info@jordanprops.co.za
www.jordanprops.co.za

Tel: 013 256 0718
Cell: 082 456 3712
E-mail: uniceann@millys.co.za

Gateway to the Lowveld

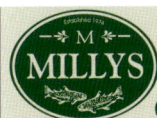

Moholoholo
The experience of a Lifetime

Tel 015 795 5236
moholorehab@wol.co.za

phalaborwa.birdclub@gmail.com
www.phalaborwa.birdclub.co.za

SbS Consultants cc
Bridging the gap between People and Systems

Business Process Design & Implementation, Change Management, Access Control, Time-&-Attendance, Project Management

Cell: 082 885 0888   achris@telkomsa.net

tshukudugamelodge@radioactivewifi.co.za
www.tshukudulodge.co.za

Adventure & Training Camp for Groups
Cell: 082 787 4280
info@adverta.co.za
www.adverta.co.za
(Nylstroom-Modimolle in Waterberg)

Spotter's Guide to
Birds of the Lowveld

S C Kidson & H L van Niekerk

Jackal Buzzard – p. 91

Contents

Introduction	3
Shapefinder	**4**
Dueldex	**8**
How to use the guide	11
Species sections	**14**
Rare visitors to the Lowveld	208
Vagrants to the Lowveld	210
Underwing Patterns	212
Immature Birds	215
Birdlife South Africa and other institutions	217
Glossary	218
Acknowledgements	219
Bibliography	220
About the authors	221
Lowveld map – inside back cover	

A project of

Blue Crane Heritage
Training and Projects
CC 1992/032772/23

P O Box 1886
Naboomspruit 0560 RSA
e-mail: info@adverta.co.za
web: www.adverta.co.za

Published by
Briza Publications
CC 1990/011690/23

P O Box 11050
Queenswood 0121
Pretoria, South Africa
web: www.briza.co.za

Other publications by the authors: Spotter's Guide to Birds of the Bushveld

---

Front cover photograph Martial Eagle by Myburgh Kennekam, background photograph Archie van Reenen, back cover photograph Southern Ground-Hornbill by Willem Frost
Copyright © in text: the authors
Copyright © in the terms "Shapefinder" and "Dueldex": the authors
Copyright © in photographs and drawings: individual photographers and artists
Copyright © in published edition: Briza Publications

© All rights reserved. No portion of this publication may be reproduced or transferred in any form or by any means without the written consent of the copyright holder.

ISBN 978-1-875093-90-8
First edition, first impression 2009, Second edition, first impression 2011
Also available in Afrikaans (ISBN 978-1-875093-91-5)
Cover design, layout and translation: Adverta Media Services
(www.adverta.co.za)
Reproduction preparation: Estelle Schoeman Cosmo Design
coscentp@worldonline.co.za
Printed and bound by Craft Print International Ltd, Singapore

Introduction

Bird watching, especially by enthusiastic novices, is presently one of the fastest growing pastimes in the world. The reason for this is not only the healthy relaxation and exercise that it offers in the freedom of nature, but the added benefit that man can enhance his own knowledge about nature and can also contribute, in a small and humble way, to our scientific knowledge.

The Lowveld of South Africa, which is home to arguably the most well-known and popular game reserve in the world, the Kruger National Park, is to a large extent still unspoilt and the peaceful home of its exceptionally rich birdlife. With its large variety of accommodation establishments the Lowveld offers easy access to these unique and beautiful birding assets.

The Spotter's Guide to Birds of the Lowveld is the second bird field guide in the series of South African regional bird guides, following on the *Spotter's Guide to Birds of the Bushveld*. All the birds of the Lowveld are described in it for easy identification by two of South Africa's most distinguished birders.

Various good bird books are available in South Africa. What makes this *Spotter's Guide* so exceptional, is its handy pocket size and all weather cover, its unique **Shapefinder** for form identification and the **Dueldex** bilingual index which allows for exceptionally quick navigation and bird identification.

The *Spotter's Guide to Birds of the Lowveld* is welcomed as one guide that can easily unlock the wonders of the natural birdlife of the Lowveld for each visitor, be it young or old, amateur or scientist, South African or overseas tourist. It deserves a well-earned place in each vehicle, in each backpack and on every bookshelf.

Dr Salomon Joubert
Park Warden – Kruger National Park
1987 to 1994

From the authors

The success and popularity of *Spotter's Guide to Birds of the Bushveld* inspired us to continue with and complete this second book in the important series of new and innovative bird publications ahead of schedule. As with the first book it is once again a monument to our various contributors and especially our wildlife photographer friends from all over the world. Without them this book would not have been possible. We honour them.

May this book become your most reliable and favourite field companion. Enjoy!

Saartjie Kidson & Herman van Niekerk
November 2008

Bird Shapefinder© 1

Group 1: Cormorant-like

Long necks, strong bills

Cormorant
Darter
Finfoot

Fresh water 14 - 15

Group 1: Duck-like

Webbed feet, oval bodies

Duck
Goose
Grebe

Fresh water 16 - 20

Group 1: Gull-like

Webbed feet, elongated bodies

Gull
Tern

Fresh water 21

Group 1: Kingfisher

Sharp bills longer than heads

Kingfisher

Fresh water 22 - 24

Group 1: Plover-like

Usually short legs and short black pointed bills

Plovers   Stint
Turnstone   Sanderling
Sandpiper   Ruff

Fresh water 25 - 29

Group 1: Special adaptations for feeding

Unusual heads & bills

Pelican   Flamingo
Hamerkop   Snipe
Spoonbill

Fresh water 29 - 31

Group 1: Stilt-like

Waders, long legs, long thin bills

Greenshank
Avocet
Stilt

Fresh water 32

Group 2: Heron-like

Large, long necks, some with long legs

Heron   Bittern
Egret   Stork
Night-Heron   Ibis

Wetland 33 - 41

Group 2: Moorhen-like

Long-toed birds

Rail   Gallinule
Crake   Moorhen
Flufftail   Coot
Swamphen   Jacana

Wetland 42 - 47

Bird Shapefinder© 2

Group 3: Crane

Long necks, long black legs

Crane

Veld 48

Group 3: Dove-like

Dove-shaped birds

Pigeon
Dove
Sandgrouse

Veld 49 - 54

Group 3: Fowl-like

Fowl-like birds

Francolin
Spurfowl
Guineafowl
Quail
Buttonquail

Veld 54 - 57

Group 3: Korhaan-like

Tall birds, long legs

Bustard
Korhaan
Ostrich

Veld 58 - 59

Group 3: Lapwing-like

Smaller birds, long legs

Thick-knee
Courser
Lapwing

Veld 60 - 63

Group 3: LBJ's

Very small, dull brown grey & black birds

Cisticola	Longclaw
Grassbird	Wagtail
Lark	Warbler
Pipit	

Veld 64 - 81

Group 4: Eagle-like

Large raptors, beaks hooked, talons

Secretarybird	Snake-Eagle
Kite	Fish-eating
Allied species	raptors
Eagle	Buzzard

Prey 82 - 91

Group 4: Falcon-like

Smaller raptors, beaks hooked, talons

Goshawk	Harrier
Sparrowhawk	Falcon
Harrier-Hawk	Kestrel

Prey 92 - 101

Group 4: Owl

Forward-looking large eyes, talons

Owl

Prey 102 - 105

Bird Shapefinder© 3

Group 5: Vulture

Strong hooked beaks, talons

Vulture

Scavengers   106-107

Group 6: Sunbird-like

Small birds, slender curved bills

Sugarbird
Sunbird

Nectar feeders   108-111

Group 7: Adapted bills

Fairly heavy adapted bills

Coucal
Crow & Raven
Oxpecker
Honeyguide
Honeybird

Unusual feeders 112-116

Group 8: Sparrow-like

Short conical bills

Bunting
Canary
Sparrow

Seed eaters   116-121

Group 8: Weaver-like

Sharp pointed bills

Bishop
Weaver & Quelea
True Weavers
Widow
Whydah

Seed eaters   122-132

Group 8: Waxbill-like

Very small birds

Finch   Mannikin
Firefinch   Pytilia (Melba)
Indigobird   Twinspot
               Waxbill

Seed eaters   133-141

Group 9: Barbet-like

Strong heavy bills

Barbet
Tinkerbird
Roller

Mixed feeders 142-145

Group 9: Parrot

Strong broad curved bills

Parrot

Mixed feeders   145-146

Group 9: Prominent crests

Mostly prominent crests

Bulbul   Mousebird
Brownbul   Trogon
Greenbul   Turaco
Nicator   Go-away-Bird

Mixed feeders 147-151

Bird Shapefinder© 4

Group 10: Batis-like

Small birds, prominent features

Apalis
Batis & Wattle-eye
Camaroptera
Crombec
Eremomela
Penduline-Tit
Prinia
Tit-Babbler
White-eye
Wren-Warbler

Insect eating   152-160

Group 10: Thrush-like

Small bills, rock & ground birds

Chat
Robin
Thrush
Wheatear

Insect eating   161-169

Group 10: Hoopoe-like

Small-medium birds, slender curved bills

Bee-eater
Hoopoe
Wood-Hoopoe

Insect eating   170-172

Group 10: Hornbill

Curved and heavy bills

Hornbill
Ground-Hornbill

Insect eating   173-174

Group 10: Nightjar

Short bills, wide gape, large eyes

Nightjar

Insect eating   175-176

Group 10: Oriole-like

Medium birds, straight bills

Babbler
Cuckooshrike
Drongo
Oriole
Woodpecker
Wryneck

Insect eating   177-182

Group 10: Shrike-like

Small-medium birds, curved & hooked bills

Cuckoo
Shrike

Insect eating   183-191

Group 10: Starling-like

Small birds, slender bills

Bush-Shrike
Broadbill
Hyliota
Flycatcher
Starling
Tit

Insect eating   191-199

Group 10: Swallow-like

Mostly aerial birds

Martin
Swallow
Saw-wing
Swift
Spinetail
Pratincole

Insect eating   200-207

7

Dueldex©
Bilingual index of group and some individual names.

P.	Name	P.	Name
106	Aasvoël/Vulture (208)	60	Dikkop/Thick-knee
152	Apalis/Kleinjantjie	20	Dobbertjie/Grebe (208)
85	Arend/Eagle	49	Dove/Duif/Duifie (211)
32	Avocet/Elsie	182	Draaihals/Wryneck
133	Baardmannetjie/Finch	61	Drawwertjie/Courser
177	Babbler/Katlagter	16	Duck/Eend (208) (210)
142	Barbet/Houtkapper	49	Duif/Dove/Pigeon (211)
89	Bateleur/Berghaan	52	Duifie/Duif/Wood-Dove
153	Batis/Bosbontrokkie	14	Duiker/Cormorant
170	Bee-eater/Byvreter	179	Drongo/Byvanger
89	Berghaan/Bateleur	-	Dunlin/Strandloper (210)
-	Berglyster/Chat (211)	85	Eagle/Arend
122	Bishop/Vink/Flap	16	Eend/Duck/Shoveler/Pochard (208) (210)
37	Bittern/Rietreier/Woudapie	-	Eend/Pintail/Garganey (210)
-	Blackcap/Tiptol (209)	34	Egret/Reier (208)
46	Bleshoender/Coot	32	Elsie/Avocet/Stilt
83	Blouvalk/Kite	156	Eremomela/Bossanger
136	Blouvinkie/Indigobird	98	Falcon/Valk (208)
190	Bokmakierie	133	Finch/Vink/Baardmannetjie
162	Bontrokkie/Stonechat	15	Finfoot/Watertrapper
153	Bosbontrokkie/Batis/Wattle-eye	135	Firefinch/Vuurvinkie
173	Boskraai/Hornbill	187	Fiscal/Laksman
147	Boskrapper/Brownbul	55	Fisant/Spurfowl
148	Boskruiper/Greenbul	90	Fish-Eagle/Visarend
192	Boslaksman/Bush-Shrike	30	Flamingo/Flamink
150	Bosloerie/Trogon	30	Flamink/Flamingo
-	Bosmusikant/Weaver (210)	123	Flap/Bishop
156	Bossanger/Eremomela	129	Flap/Widowbird
188	Boubou/Waterfiskaal	44	Flufftail/Vleikuiken
193	Breëbek/Broadbill	193	Flycatcher/Vlieëvanger (209)
193	Broadbill/Breëbek	-	Fraiingpoot/Phalarope (209) (211)
174	Bromvoël/Ground-Hornbill	54	Francolin/Patrys/Swempie
147	Brownbul/Boskrapper	137	Fret/Mannikin
189	Brubru/Laksman	45	Gallinule/Koningriethaan
147	Bulbul/Tiptol	19	Gans/Goose
116	Bunting/Streepkoppie	-	Garganey/Eend (210)
190	Bush-Shrike/Spookvoël/Konkoit/Boslaksman	159	Glasogie/White-eye
58	Bustard/Gompou/Korhaan	151	Go-away-bird/Kwêvoël
57	Buttonquail/Kwarteltjie	58	Gompou/Bustard
91	Buzzard/Jakkalsvoël/Valk (208)	19	Goose/Gans/Makou
179	Byvanger/Drongo	94	Goshawk/Sperwer/Singvalk
170	Byvreter/Bee-eater	68	Grassbird/Grasvoël
154	Camaroptera/Kwêkwêvoël	68	Grasvoël/Grassbird
118	Canary/Kanarie	20	Grebe/Dobbertjie (208)
-	Chat/Berglyster (211)	148	Greenbul/Willie/Boskruiper
162	Chat/Piek/Spekvreter	32	Greenshank/Ruiter
64	Cisticola/Klopkloppie/Tinktinkie	174	Ground-Hornbill/Bromvoël
161	Cliff-Chat/Dassievoël/Wagter	56	Guineafowl/Tarentaal
46	Coot/Bleshoender	21	Gull/Meeu
14	Cormorant/Duiker	41	Hadeda/Ibis
112	Coucal/Vleiloerie	30	Hamerkop
61	Courser/Drawwertjie	97	Harrier/Vleivalk
42	Crake/Riethaan/Kwartelkoning (209)	96	Harrier-Hawk/Kaalwangvalk
48	Crane/Kraanvoël/Mahem (208)	84	Hawk/Valk
155	Crombec/Stompstert	88	Hawk-Eagle/Jagarend
113	Crow/Raven/Kraai	190	Helmet-Shrike/Helmlaksman
183	Cuckoo/Koekoek (211)	190	Helmlaksman/Helmet-Shrike
178	Cuckooshrike/Katakoeroe	33	Heron/Reier
15	Darter/Slanghalsvoël	116	Heuningvoël/Honeybird
161	Dassievoël/Chat	115	Heuningwyser/Honeyguide
186	Diederikkie/Cuckoo	98	Hobby/Valk

8

P.	Name	P.	Name
172	Hoephoep/Hoopoe	199	Mees/Tit
116	Honeybird/Heuningvoël	21	Meeu/Gull
84	Honey-Buzzard/Wespedief	186	Meitjie/Cuckoo
115	Honeyguide/Heuningwyser	138	Melba/Pytilia
172	Hoopoe/Hoephoep	185	Mooimeisie/Cuckoo
173	Hornbill/Neushoringvoël/Boskraai	46	Moorhen/Waterhoender
142	Houtkapper/Barbet	120	Mossie/Sparrow/Petronia
193	Hyliota	149	Mousebird/Muisvoël
40	Ibis/Skoorsteenveër/Ibis/Hadeda	149	Muisvoël/Mousebird
136	Indigobird/Blouvinkie	197	Myna/Spreeu
47	Jacana/Langtoon	37	Nagreier/Night-Heron
88	Jagarend/Hawk-Eagle	175	Naguil/Nightjar
91	Jakkalsvoël/Buzzard (208)	68	Neddicky/Neddikkie
163	Janfrederik/Robin-Chat/Robin	68	Neddikkie/Neddicky
109	Jangroentjie/Sunbird	173	Neushoringvoël/Hornbill
96	Kaalwangvalk/Harrier-Hawk	148	Nicator/Nikator
172	Kakelaar/Wood-Hoopoe/Scimitarbill	37	Night-Heron/Nagreier
75	Kalkoentjie/Longclaw	175	Nightjar/Naguil
118	Kanarie/Canary/Seedeater	148	Nikator/Nicator
157	Kapokvoël/Penduline-Tit	40	Nimmersat/Stork
178	Katakoeroe/Cuckooshrike	184	Nuwejaarsvoël/Cuckoo
177	Katlagter/Babbler	201	Oewerswael/Martin
29	Kemphaan/Ruff	38	Ooievaar/Stork/Openbill
100	Kestrel/Valk	39	Openbill/Ooievaar
62	Kiewiet/Lapwing (209)	180	Oriole/Wielewaal
22	Kingfisher/Visvanger (211)	90	Osprey/Visvalk
83	Kite/Wou/Blouvalk	59	Ostrich/Volstruis
70	Klappertjie/Lark	102	Owl/Uil
152	Kleinjantjie/Apalis	114	Oxpecker/Renostervoël
168	Kliplyster/Rock-Thrush	145	Papegaai/Parrot
64	Klopkloppie/Cisticola	145	Parrot/Papegaai
183	Koekoek/Cuckoo (211)	55	Patrys/Francolin
72	Koester/Pipit (210) (211)	29	Pelican/Pelikaan
139	Kolpensie/Twinspot	29	Pelikaan/Pelican
45	Koningriethaan/Swamphen/Gallinule	157	Penduline-Tit/Kapokvoël
191	Konkoit/Bush-Shrike	121	Petronia/Mossie
58	Korhaan/Bustard	-	Phalarope/Fraaiingpoot (209) (211)
123	Koringvoël/Sparrow-Weaver	162	Piek/Chat
113	Kraai/Crow/Raven	184	Piet-my-vrou/Cuckoo
-	Kraanvoël/Crane (208)	49	Pigeon/Duif
57	Kwartel/Quail	-	Pintail/Eend (210)
42	Kwartelkoning/Crake	72	Pipit/Koester (210) (211)
57	Kwarteltjie/Buttonquail	-	Pitta (211)
154	Kwêkwêvoël/Camaroptera	25	Plover/Strandkiewiet (210)
124	Kwelea/Quelea	18	Pochard/Eend
151	Kwêvoël/Go-away-bird	207	Pratincole/Sprinkaanvoël
76	Kwikkie/Wagtail	158	Prinia/Langstertjie
187	Laksman/Shrike/Fiscal/Brubru	189	Puffback/Sneeubal
158	Langstertjie/Prinia	138	Pytilia/Melba
47	Langtoon/Jacana	57	Quail/Kwartel
62	Lapwing/Kiewiet (209)	124	Quelea/Kwelea
69	Lark/Lewerik/Klappertjie	42	Rail/Riethaan
30	Lepelaar/Spoonbill	114	Raven/Kraai
69	Lewerik/Lark/Sparrowlark	-	Redshank/Ruiter (210)
151	Loerie/Turaco	33	Reier/Heron/Egret (208)
75	Longclaw/Kalkoentjie	114	Renostervoël/Oxpecker
166	Lyster/Thrush	42	Riethaan/Rail/Crake (209)
77	Lysternagtegaal/Thrush Nightingale	37	Rietreier/Bittern
48	Mahem/Crane (208)	163	Robin-Chat/Robin/Janfrederik
20	Makou/Goose	168	Rock-Thrush/Kliplyster
137	Mannikin/Fret	144	Roller/Troupant
40	Maraboe/Marabou Stork	141	Rooiassie/Waxbill
40	Marabou Stork/Maraboe	131	Rooibekkie/Whydah (210)
96	Marsh-Harrier/Vleivalk	29	Ruff/Kemphaan
200	Martin/Swael/Oewerswael	27	Ruiter/Sandpiper (209)
		32	Ruiter/Greenshank/Redshank (210)
		28	Sanderling/Strandkiewiet

9

P.	Name	P.	Name
53	Sandgrouse/Sandpatrys	17	Teal/Eend
53	Sandpatrys/Sandgrouse	21	Tern/Sterretjie (211)
27	Sandpiper/Ruiter/Strandloper (209) (210)	60	Thick-knee/Dikkop
		166	Thrush/Lyster
78	Sanger/Warbler/Whitethroat (209) (211)	77	Thrush Nightingale/Lysternagtegaal
155	Sanger/Woodland-Warbler	143	Tinker/Tinkerbird
160	Sanger/Wren-Warbler	143	Tinkerbird/Tinker
204	Saw-wing/Swael	66	Tinktinkie/Cisticola
172	Scimitarbill/Kakelaar	147	Tiptol/Bulbul/Blackcap (209)
103	Scops-Owl/Uil	199	Tit/Mees
164	Scrub-Robin/Wipstert	159	Tit-Babbler/Tjeriktik
82	Secretarybird/Sekretarisvoël	189	Tjagra/Tchagra
120	Seedeater/Kanarie	159	Tjeriktik/Tit-Babbler
82	Sekretarisvoël/Secretarybird	150	Trogon/Bosloerie
18	Shoveler/Eend	144	Troupant/Roller
93	Shrika/Sperwer	151	Turaco/Loerie
187	Shrike/Laksman	27	Turnstone/Steenloper
94	Singvalk/Goshawk	139	Twinspot/Kolpensie
40	Skoorsteenveër/Ibis	102	Uil/Owl/Scops-Owl
89	Slangarend/Snake-Eagle	84	Valk/Hawk
15	Slanghalsvoël/Darter	98	Valk/Falcon/Hobby/Kestrel (208)
89	Snake-Eagle/Slangarend	122	Vink/Bishop
189	Sneeubal/Puffback	126	Vink/Weaver
31	Snip/Snipe	132	Vink/Whydah/Finch (210)
31	Snipe/Snip	134	Vinkie/Finch
120	Sparrow/Mossie	90	Visarend/Fish-Eagle
92	Sparrowhawk/Sperwer	90	Visvalk/Osprey
71	Sparrowlark/Lewerik	22	Visvanger/Kingfisher (211)
123	Sparrow-Weaver/Koringvoël	44	Vleikuiken/Flufftail
181	Speg/Woodpecker	112	Vleiloerie/Coucal
161	Spekvreter/Chat	96	Vleivalk/Marsh-Harrier
92	Sperwer/Sparrowhawk/Shrika/Goshawk	193	Vlieëvanger/Flycatcher (209)
		59	Volstruis/Ostrich
207	Spinetail/Stekelstert	106	Vulture/Aasvoël (208)
190	Spookvoël/Bush-Shrike	135	Vuurvinkie/Firefinch
30	Spoonbill/Lepelaar	76	Wagtail/Kwikkie
197	Spreeu/Starling/Myna (209) (211)	169	Wagter/Wheatear/Chat
207	Sprinkaanvoël/Pratincole	78	Warbler/Sanger (209) (211)
55	Spurfowl/Fisant	188	Waterfiskaal/Boubou
197	Starling/Spreeu (209) (211)	46	Waterhoender/Moorhen
27	Steenloper/Turnstone	15	Watertrapper/Finfoot
207	Stekelstert/Spinetail	154	Wattle-eye/Bosbontrokkie
21	Sterretjie/Tern (211)	140	Waxbill/Rooiassie/Swie/Sysie
32	Stilt/Elsie	123	Weaver/Wewer/Vink
28	Stint/Strandloper	84	Wespedief/Honey-Buzzard
155	Stompstert/Crombec	123	Wewer/Weaver/Bosmusikant (210)
162	Stonechat/Bontrokkie	169	Wheatear/Wagter
38	Stork/Ooievaar/Nimmersat	-	Whimbrel/Wulp (211)
25	Strandkiewiet/Plover (210)	159	White-eye/Glasogie
28	Strandkiewiet/Sanderling	78	Whitethroat/Sanger
-	Strandloper/Dunlin (210)	131	Whydah/Rooibekkie/Vink (210)
28	Strandloper/Sandpiper/Stint (209) (210)	129	Widowbird/Flap
116	Streepkoppie/Bunting	180	Wielewaal/Oriole
108	Sugarbird/Suikervoël	148	Willie/Greenbul
109	Suikerbekkie/Sunbird (209)	205	Windswael/Swift
108	Suikervoël/Sugarbird	164	Wipstert/Scrub-Robin
109	Sunbird/Suikerbekkie/Jangroentjie (209)	52	Wood-Dove/Duifie
		172	Wood-Hoopoe/Kakelaar
200	Swael/Swallow/Saw-wing/Martin	155	Woodland-Warbler/Sanger
202	Swallow/Swael	181	Woodpecker/Speg
45	Swamphen/Koningriethaan	83	Wou/Kite
54	Swempie/Francolin	37	Woudapie/Bittern
141	Swie/Waxbill	160	Wren-Warbler/Sanger
205	Swift/Windswael	182	Wryneck/Draaihals
140	Sysie/Waxbill	-	Wulp/Whimbrel (211)
56	Tarentaal/Guineafowl		
189	Tchagra/Tjagra		

How to use this Spotter's Guide©

In this guide birds are grouped together according to outward appearance. Identify the group of birds you are looking for from the **Bird Shapefinder** on pages **4** to **7**. Turn to the pages listed for that group of birds. Distinguishing characteristics of each bird are included in the guide as icons or text. By using the legend described in this section of the guide, general information related to identifying each bird can be obtained. The male bird in breeding plumage is normally depicted and described in this guide.

Know the most important bird terms that we refer to:

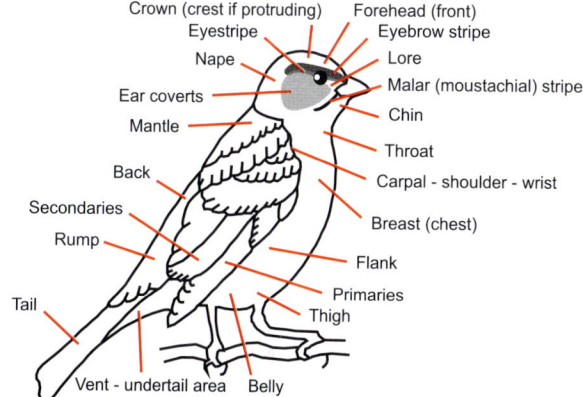

Crown (crest if protruding)
Forehead (front)
Eyestripe
Eyebrow stripe
Nape
Lore
Malar (moustachial) stripe
Ear coverts
Chin
Mantle
Throat
Back
Carpal - shoulder - wrist
Secondaries
Breast (chest)
Rump
Flank
Primaries
Tail
Thigh
Vent - undertail area
Belly

Interpret the layout (14 sets of information):

① Bird's reference number
② What time of year to look for bird. Diamond indicates exotic bird
③ Bird's normal habitat. Triangle indicates bird of higher altitudes
④ General size of bird
⑤ Bird's social behaviour
⑥ Main food sources
⑦ Where to locate bird's nest: P = parasitic; X = not breeding in South Africa
⑧ Prominent visual feature
⑨ Common English and Afrikaans names
⑩ Acknowledgement of photographic source
⑪ Remarks to assist identification
⑫ Photo (drawing if rare)
⑬ Sex of bird
⑭ Group (10 colour-coded strips)

Crested Francolin / Bospatrys
Black beak; yellowish eye; reddish eyering

11

① **Bird's reference number.**

② **What time of year to look for bird.**

All year presence	Summer visitor to South Africa	Winter visitor to Lowveld	Exotic species introduced into South Africa
A	**S**	**W**	♦

③ **Bird's normal habitat.**
Indicates the environment where the bird is most likely to be found.

 Plains, open grass field, savanna

 Scrub & shrub areas

 Predominantly thorn tree veld

 Valleys & gorges

 Predominantly broad-leaved tree veld

 Mountains, slopes, cliffs, rock faces

 Forest & dense bush, forest fringes

 Drier areas or locations

 Riverine woodland

 Urban gardens, parks, cultivated land & areas of human habitation

 Water (dams, rivers, reeds, streams, wooded streams, marshes, vleiland)

Virtually all habitats

▲ Triangle on habitat icon indicates bird frequents higher altitudes.

④ **Bird's size.**
General size of bird according to its weight (therefore the graphic of a scale in the icon) and not according to its length or height, which may be misleading. Birds indicated as Very Small, Small, Small to Medium, Medium, Medium to Large, Large and Very Large.

VS   S   SM   M   ML   L   VL

- VS – 6 - 20 g – Penduline-Tit, Cisticola, Waxbill, Canary.
- S – 21 - 50 g – Tit, Robin, Swallow, Flycatcher, Pipit, Lark.
- SM – 51 - 100 g – Kingfisher, Thrush, Shrike, Dove.
- M – 101 - 500 g – Roller, Kingfisher, Francolin, Pigeon, Egret.
- ML – 501 g - 1 kg – Duck, Heron, Ibis, Korhaan.
- L – 1 - 5 kg – Goose, Guineafowl, Stork, Secretarybird.
- VL – 5 kg + – Vulture, Marabou, Ostrich.

⑤ **Bird's social behaviour.**

Bird's social behaviour indicated as usually found as solitary, in pairs, in small groups, in family groups (gregarious), in flocks or in swarms.

⑥ **Main food source of group, although other food may also be taken.**

Seeds	Fish, fish fry & crabs	Medium sized mammals
Fruit, berries & blossoms	Tadpoles & frogs	Hares, rabbits, hyraxes
Insects, worms & similar	Reptiles (snakes, lizards, geckoes)	Nectar from flowers
Grass & plant material	Snails, molluscs	Honey & beeswax
Rodents, smaller mammals	Bird & other eggs	Ticks & parasites
Water life, crustaceans	Birds & bird chicks	Carrion & waste

⑦ **Where to locate bird's nest.**
Egg in icon indicates nest as being on or at **water**, on **ground**, attached to **grass or reeds**, in **shrubs**, in **trees**, on **mountains and cliffs**, in **hollow tree trunks**, in **sand banks or in the ground** or on/in **man-made structures such as bridges, buildings and pylons** (D for Domestic). The P-icon indicates that the bird is parasitic and an X-icon that it does not breed in South Africa. A + indicates communal breeding.

+ = communal breeder

⑧ **Very prominent visual identification feature.**

Photograph or sketch

⑨ **Bird's common English and Afrikaans names.**

⑩ **Identification of photographer or photographic source.**

⑪ **Some distinguishing habits or traits to look for.**

⑫ **Photograph (or drawing in event of rare bird).**

⑬ **Sexual traits.** ♀ Female   ♂ Male

⑭ **Colour guide for group identification.**

Group 1 – Fresh water
Cormorant-like

Long necks, strong beaks, swim with bodies submerged in water, dive after fish.

Cormorant has hooked beak and webbed feet.
Darter has straight beak and webbed feet.
Finfoot has straight beak and lobed feet.

White-breasted Cormorant / Witborsduiker

Black with green gloss; green eye, white chin and breast; juvenile completely white below

Reed Cormorant / Rietduiker

Glossy black; yellow bill, red eye, small crest on forehead, longish rounded tail; juv. off-white below; opens its wings to dry

14

African Darter / Slanghalsvoël

Brownish above, darker below; small head, sharp pointed bill, snaky neck, long stiff tail; wing streaks; swims low in water; opens wings to dry

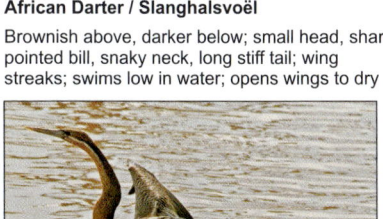

 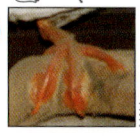

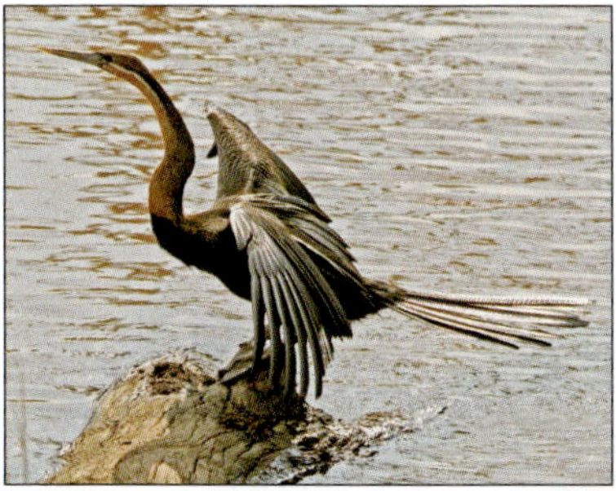

African Finfoot / Watertrapper

Elongated body; spotted dark brown back; red bill, white eyestripe, red legs and feet; large lobed toes; longish tail held flat on water; shy; scarce

Group 1 – Fresh water
Duck-like

Webbed feet, oval bodies, dependent on water sources and availability of food.

Duck
Goose
Grebe

Duck

Found at most inland water with aquatic vegetation. Will head-dip, dive and up-end for food. Powerful fliers. Some species call in flight.

White-faced Duck / Nonnetjie-eend

White face, black bill, neck and feet, rich brown back, barred below; stands very erect; nomadic; whistling duck

Fulvous Duck / Fluiteend

Copper head, dark line down back of head, black bill, cream-coloured feathers on flank; stands very erect; nomadic; shy and wary; whistling duck

White-backed Duck / Witrugeend

Round-backed; reddish-brown mottled body, pale spot at base of bill; floats low with tail under water; white back only visible during flight; whistling duck

Yellow-billed Duck / Geelbekeend

Dark bird with scaly appearance; yellow bill with dark central saddle, green speculum

African Black Duck / Swarteend

Elongated body; black bill, white spotting on back, green speculum white edged, yellow-orange legs and feet, longish tail; highly territorial; shy

Cape Teal / Teeleend

Pale grey, brownish speckled; grey head, red eye, rose-pink bill, white speculum with green edge; uncommon

17

Hottentot Teal / Gevlekte Eend

Smallish delicate duck; black cap and blue bill, spotted breast, dark back, green speculum with white edge; shy

Red-billed Teal / Rooibekeend

Smallish duck; dark above, mottled buff below; black cap, red bill, light orange speculum

Cape Shoveler / Kaapse Slopeend
Brown blotched dark brown; greyish-brown head, male yellow eye, female dark brown eye, long broad black bill, green speculum, yellow to orange feet

Southern Pochard / Bruineend

Male dark brown, red eye, pale blue bill; female lighter grey-brown with white C-mark behind the eye down to the neck; prefers deep water; seldom on land

Comb Duck / Knobbeleend

Head white and speckled, male black bill with knob when breeding, back and wings black-purple sheen, white below, black feet; female much smaller without knob

Goose

Found at inland water with aquatic vegetation.

Egyptian Goose / Kolgans

Large; dark brown above, greyish below; pink bill, chestnut circle around eyes, white wing pattern, chestnut spot on chest, red feet; stands high on legs

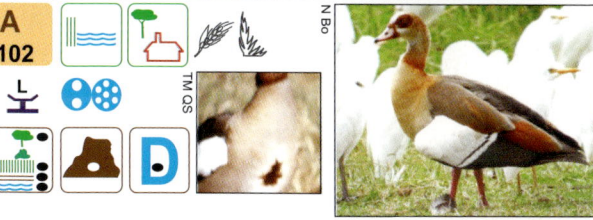

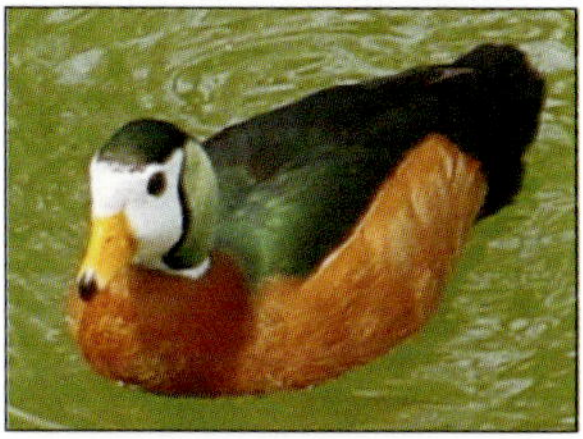

African Pygmy-Goose / Dwerggans
Small; metallic green above, chestnut below; head white, bill yellow with black tip, metallic green cap and patches on side of head, female orange below, head speckled; rare

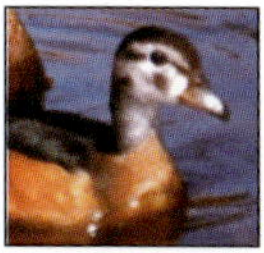

Spur-winged Goose / Wildemakou

Large; mostly black; white belly, white patches on head, pink face, bill, legs and feet, male frontal knob; female smaller

Grebe

Smallish wings, pointed beak. Legs placed far backward. Lobed feet. Virtually no tail. Masterful underwater swimmers. Walk with difficulty.

Great Crested Grebe / Kuifkopdobbertjie

Brownish above, white below; large rufous head with double black crest, red eye, white face, long neck; elaborate courting display on water

Little Grebe / Kleindobbertjie

Dark brownish bird; black cap, light-coloured patch at base of beak, chestnut cheeks and neck; non-breeding plumage drab

20

Group 1 – Fresh water
Gull-like
Webbed feet, oval bodies.

Gull – Typical seabird plumage, scavenger, robber, will eat virtually anything.
Tern – Freshwater terns with squarish tails, occur mostly on inland waters, hawking low over water and upwind for insects.

Grey-headed Gull / Gryskopmeeu

Mostly white with pale grey head; soft yellow eye with red eyering, grey wings with black tips, bright red bill and legs; imm. grey mottled above; noisy

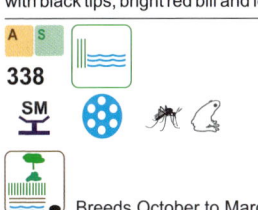

Breeds October to March

Whiskered Tern / Witbaardsterretjie

Breeding plumage black cap and white cheek, red bill, legs and feet, non-breeding mainly white with grey back and rump and speckled crown

White-winged Tern / Witvlerksterretjie

Grey back, white below; white head speckled black, dark patch behind eye, white rump; present from late August to late April

Group 1 – Fresh water
Kingfisher
Sharp beaks, longer than heads.

Mostly very colourful, especially in flight. Fast flyers. Sit still for long periods looking for prey, or hover above water. Bobs head and flicks tail before diving onto prey. Hits prey on hard object like tree trunk to kill and soften before eating. Some species found away from water.

Pied Kingfisher / Bontvisvanger

White eyebrow and chin, black eyestripe, male double breast band, female single broken breast band

Giant Kingfisher / Reusevisvanger

Largest kingfisher; black spotted white above; tightly plumed head, male rufous breast, female rufous belly

Half-collared Kingfisher / Blouvisvanger

Cobalt blue above, buffy below; black bill, white spot behind ear, red feet; rare

Malachite Kingfisher / Kuifkopvisvanger

Short body and tail; blue above, rufous below; light blue and black crown extending to eye, red bill (black in juv.), white chin and streaks on neck

African Pygmy-Kingfisher / Dwergvisvanger

Blue above, bright cinnamon below; blue banded crown, lilac ear patches, bright cinnamon eyebrow, red bill and feet; may nest in antbear hole; unobtrusive

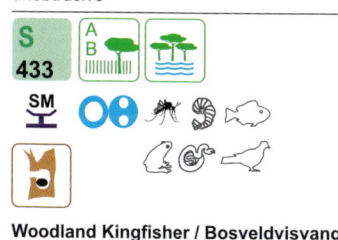

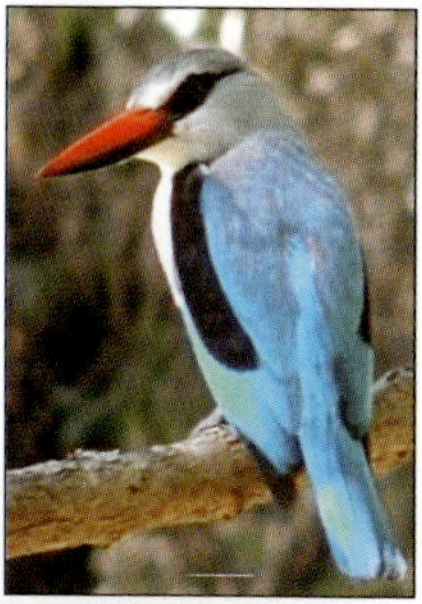

Woodland Kingfisher / Bosveldvisvanger

Turquoise above, white below; black shoulders, black eyestripe ending behind eye, bill red above, black below; voice: 5 to 10 second trill

Brown-hooded Kingfisher / Bruinkopvisvanger

Male black back, lightly striped below; red bill with black tip, striped brown crown, dark red feet, female brown back; noisy

Grey-headed Kingfisher / Gryskopvisvanger

Grey head and mantle, blue wings with black shoulder, red bill, cinnamon belly, red feet; may nest in antbear hole; rare

Striped Kingfisher / Gestreepte Visvanger

Drab; prominent black eyestripe, bill dark above and red below, white neck and cheeks, breast and flanks softly striped; voice: 1 to 2 second trill

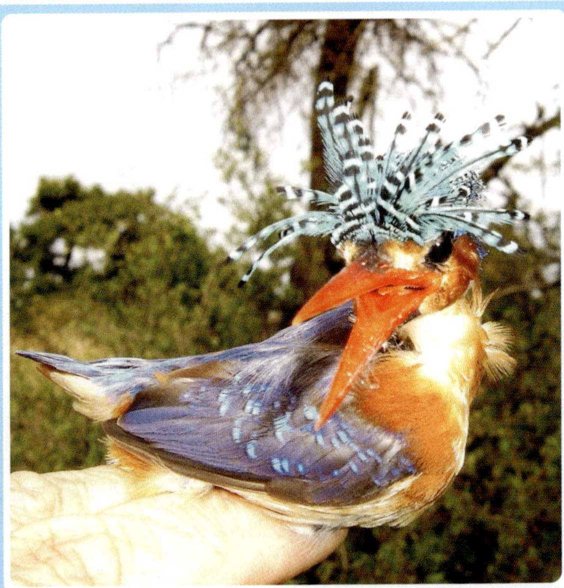

431 Alarmed

Group 1 – Fresh water
Plover-like

Waders, usually with short legs and short black pointed bills.

Plover
Turnstone
Sandpiper

Stint
Sanderling
Ruff

Resident Waders

True plovers, short pigeon-like bills, moving by intermittent runs with motionless pauses in between.

A 246

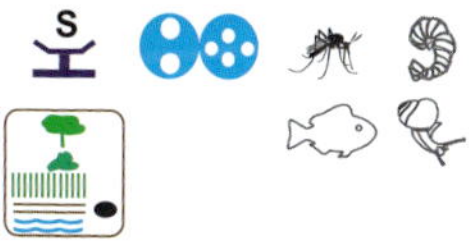

White-fronted Plover / Vaalstrandkiewiet
Pale sandy-grey wings, white below; white forehead and nape, thin black line extending through eye; runs fast with head drawn into shoulders, trembles feet in shallow water when feeding

A 247

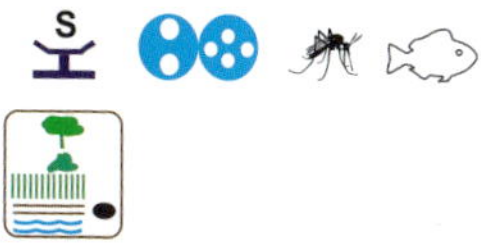

Chestnut-banded Plover / Rooibandstrandkiewiet
Hunched posture; pale grey above, white below; male black markings on forehead, black line extending through eye, narrow chestnut band across chest

25

Kittlitz's Plover / Geelborsstrandkiewiet
Breeding plumage black forehead and eyestripe extending behind eye onto nape, white throat, orange-yellow tinge on breast; female no black on head

Three-banded Plover / Driebandstrandkiewiet
Red eyering and red bill with black tip, grey cheeks, two black bands across chest, pinkish grey legs and feet, white terminal bar visible in flight

Visiting Waders

Waders visiting the Lowveld in their drab non-breeding dress.

Common Ringed Plover / Ringnekstrandkiewiet
Dark above, white below; black and white bands on head and neck, short bill mostly orange at base, short orange-yellow legs; usually quiet in South Africa; found on muddy wetlands

Termites

Caspian Plover / Asiatiese Strandkiewiet

Upright stance; wings sandy-brown, buffy-white below; broad buffy eyestripe, dull grey-brown wash across the breast; found here and there

Ruddy Turnstone / Steenloper

Stocky, long-bodied; pied head, wings blackish-brown, irregular blackish markings on bib and side of breast, white below; very short orange legs; turn stones to feed

Common Sandpiper / Gewone Ruiter

Bronzy-brown above, white below; white also forming white comma on shoulder, distinct black eyestripe, dark rump; bobs tail like a wagtail

Wood Sandpiper / Bosruiter

Dark brown-grey above clearly spotted, white below; lightly streaked on chest and throat, white eyestripe, white rump, yellow-green legs, barred tail

27

Marsh Sandpiper / Moerasruiter
Back, head and neck greyish, white below; straight and slender bill, long grey-green legs; tends to wade in deeper water; smaller than Common Greenshank (p. 32)

Curlew Sandpiper / Krombekstrandloper
Drab above, white below; longish decurved bill, shows white rump in flight; posture somewhat hunched; forages mainly on mud flats

Little Stint / Kleinstrandloper
Slender body; warmish brown tinge above, white below; short straight bill, white eyebrow

Sanderling / Drietoonstrandkiewiet
Pale grey above, white below; short stubby bill with rounded tip, short black legs; runs head down following the movement of the water; ploughs through mud

Ruff (Reeve) / Kemphaan

Brownish, scaly appearance above, white below; straight dark bill, longish legs usually light orange

Group 1 – Fresh water
Special adaptations
Unusual heads and beaks, specialised feeders.

Pelican
Hamerkop
Spoonbill

Flamingo
Snipe

Great White Pelican / Witpelikaan

Mostly white with a yellowish breast patch; very big yellow and bluish bill with yellow pouch, pink facial skin, pink to yellow legs, yellow webbed feet; hunt in ranks; nomadic

Pink-backed Pelican / Kleinpelikaan

Smaller than 49; pale grey with wash of pink; pale yellow bill with pinkish pouch, orange legs, webbed feet; hunts singly; nomadic

29

Hamerkop

Sepia brown coloured; large bill and prominent crest; shuffles feet underwater to feed; may snatch food from water in flight; massive nests

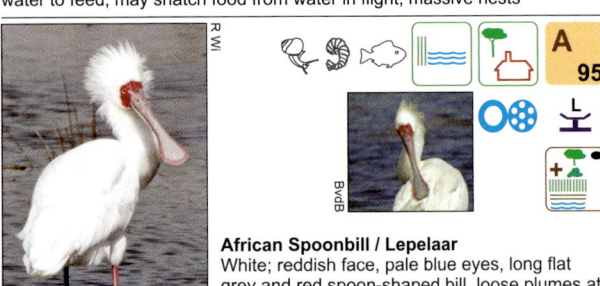

African Spoonbill / Lepelaar

White; reddish face, pale blue eyes, long flat grey and red spoon-shaped bill, loose plumes at back of head, red legs and feet; shy

Greater Flamingo / Grootflamink

White to pale pink; pale pink bill with black point, yellow eyes with pink eyering, long curved neck, scarlet upperwing, long slender reddish legs; feeds in muddy water; nomadic

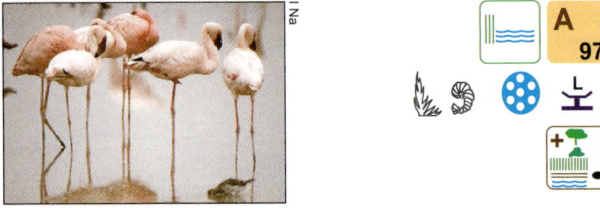

Lesser Flamingo / Kleinflamink

White to deep pink; dark maroon bill with black point, yellow-orange eyes, long neck, crimson wing coverts, long slender pinkish legs; feeds in water; nomadic

Snipe

Cryptically coloured birds with short legs and very long bills for probing in the mud in their favourite marsh habitat. Shy and retiring.

A 242

Greater Painted-snipe / Goudsnip

Male tesselated soft brownish-chestnut; thin black line between brown chest and white belly, female larger and more brightly coloured with chestnut above; white eye patch, white band across lower breast

A 286

African Snipe / Afrikaanse Snip

Striped and spotted golden brown above, white below barred on chest and flanks; head striped, very long bill, shortish legs; remarkable courtship flights

31

Group 1 – Fresh water
Stilt-like
Waders, long thin beaks, long legs.

Greenshank
Avocet
Stilt

Common Greenshank / Groenpootruiter

Slate grey above, white below; slightly upturned greyish black bill; wades quickly; bobs when alarmed; shy and wary; call "chew-chew-chew"

Pied Avocet / Bontelsie

Black and white bird; black cap and nape, red eye, long very thin upturned black bill, long grey legs; feeds with side-to-side bill movement

Black-winged Stilt / Rooipootelsie

Black wings, white below; white head, red eye, thin pointed needle-like black bill, very long pink legs

32

Group 2 – Wetland
Heron-like

Large birds, long bills, long necks, some with long legs.

Heron
Egret
Night-Heron

Bittern
Stork
Ibis

Large Herons

Large birds, plumes on head; neck folded away into breast; legs stretched out behind when flying.

A 62

Grey Heron / Bloureier

Greyish bird; white crown with black band above the eye ending in a black plume, yellow bill, black patch on shoulder, grey underwing

A 63

Black-headed Heron / Swartkopreier

Slate-grey, darker above; black cap on head and down neck, dark bill and legs, in flight underwing white in front, black behind; not water dependent

33

Goliath Heron / Reusereier

Slate and chestnut coloured; chestnut crown and neck, dark bill and legs, black feet; slow flier

Purple Heron / Rooireier

Smaller and slimmer heron; above brownish-grey, dark crown, rufous neck with black throat stripes; shy

Egrets
(White Herons)

Egrets are smaller all-white herons with medium long necks, bills and legs and usually with ornamental plumes. Most are colonial breeders.

Great Egret / Grootwitreier

Long neck usually kinked; long heavy black bill when breeding (non-breeding yellow), eye red when breeding (non-breeding yellow), narrow line between the eye from gape to back of eye, black legs; shy and solitary

34

A 67

Little Egret / Kleinwitreier

Long and slim; black bill, black legs and yellow feet, full plumes when breeding; active hunter dashing to and fro in shallow water

A 68

Yellow-billed Egret / Geelbekwitreier

Bill yellow, legs above "knee" yellow, lower legs and feet black, at beginning of breeding season red bill and legs and handsome plumes

A 71

Cattle Egret / Veereier

Short yellow bill, breeding birds have reddish bill and light rufous-brown plumes on head; follows animals or perches on their backs

35

Black Heron

Folds wings over head to form umbrella to assist in detecting prey.

A 69

Black Heron / Swartreier

Black with slate-grey tinge; thin black bill, head with plumes, yellow eyes, black legs, chrome-yellow toes

Pond Herons

Sharp bills. Shorter legs than other herons. Mostly shy and skulking, partly or completely nocturnal. Some escape observation by protruding neck upwards in typical erect bittern stance.

A 72

Squacco Heron / Ralreier

Rufous brown back and neck; long white and black plumes, blue bill (black tip when breeding), yellowish legs, prominent white underwings in flight

Green-backed Heron / Groenrugreier

Mostly grey-green above; bill black above, yellow below, yellow eye, yellow lore when breeding, white throat with central rufous-brown streaks, scaly pattern on wings, yellow legs, juvenile streaked brown and buff

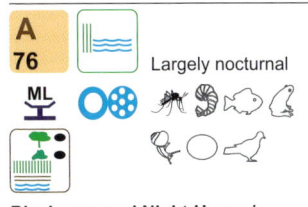

Largely nocturnal

Black-crowned Night-Heron / Gewone Nagreier

Stockily built; black above, white below; white head with black crown, black bill, red eye, yellow legs and feet, head plumes when breeding

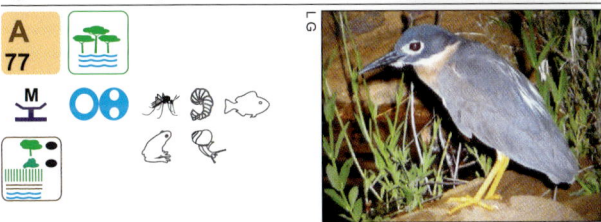

White-backed Night-Heron / Witrugnagreier

Dark head; big brown eye with white eye patch, black bill, white chin, rufous neck, grey-brown wings, soft rufous below; secretive; scarce

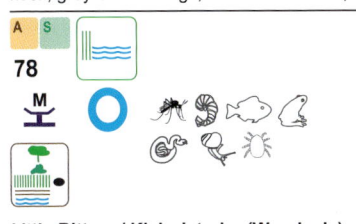

Little Bittern / Kleinrietreier (Woudapie)

Long thick neck; black cap, yellowish beak, yellow-brown on wings, buff below, female striped and mottled

Dwarf Bittern / Dwergrietreier

Dark slate above, light buff below, heavily streaked; red-brown eye, yellow legs; breeds in flooded trees and bushes

Stork

Differ from herons in having shorter toes. Fly with necks fully stretched. Silent birds; have no voice muscles; communicate by rattling bills.

Small breeding colonies in Cape

White Stork / Witooievaar

White bird with black flight feathers; red bill and legs, white tail; soars well, spiralling high on thermals

Black Stork / Grootswartooievaar

Glossy black bird with white belly and undertail, red bill and skin around the eye, red legs

38

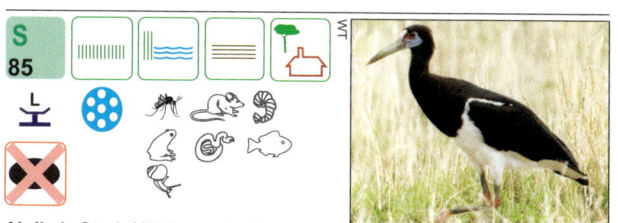

Abdim's Stork / Kleinswartooievaar

Smallest stork; black above and on upper breast, white belly and rump forming white C around front of wing; greenish-grey bill, blue cheeks, pink "knees" and feet, large flocks

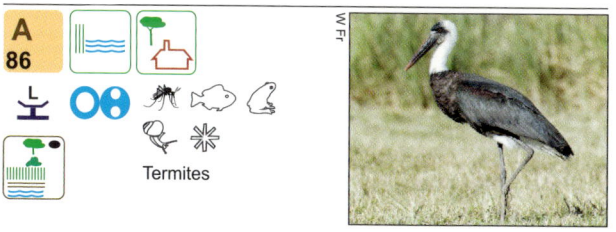

Woolly-necked Stork / Wolnekooievaar

Black above, white on belly; bill black with red tip, black eye patch, red eyes, white woolly neck, deeply forked black tail

African Openbill / Oopbekooievaar
Glossy brown-black; long heavy horn-coloured bill with a distinctive gap between the two mandibles, eyes brown with yellow inner ring, legs and feet black

Saddle-billed Stork / Saalbekooievaar
Black and white; long neck; long black and red bill with yellow saddle, pink "knees" and toes, male black eye and chin wattles, female yellow eye; shy

39

Marabou Stork / Maraboe
Slaty back, white below; naked pink head and neck with inflatable pouch, big horn-coloured bill, legs covered white; head tucked into shoulders in flight

Yellow-billed Stork / Nimmersat

White with black on wings and tail; red face, large yellow bill slightly curved down at tip, red legs; sometimes hunts with one wing raised

Ibis

Ibises are related to storks but are smaller with shorter legs and long down-curved bills.

African Sacred Ibis / Skoorsteenveër

White plumage; bare black head and neck, black back plumes, scarlet underwing during breeding, immature has white feathered neck

40

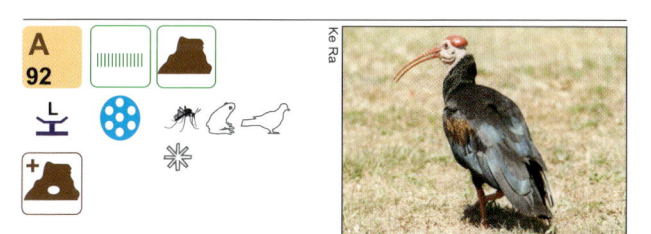

Southern Bald Ibis / Kalkoenibis

Dark glossy green with coppery wing patch; bare prominent red head and bill, white face, chin and front neck, pink legs

Glossy Ibis / Glansibis

Head, neck and body dark chestnut, back and wings with metallic green shine; slender bill, legs light brown

Hadeda Ibis / Hadeda

Greyish-brown plumage with metallic pink and bronze reflections; black bill with red ridge on upper mandible; loud call from which name is derived

41

Group 2 – Wetland
Moorhen-like

Mostly long-toed birds walking on floating plants and flying with dangling legs; good swimmers.

Rail – longer bill
Crake
Flufftail
Swamphen

Gallinule
Moorhen
Coot
Jacana

Rail and Crake

Most are skulking birds living in marshy areas or long grass; very vocal during breeding season.

African Rail / Grootriethaan
Slaty with brown back; long red bill, red eye, black and white stripes on the flanks, white undertail feathers, red legs; jerky movement with a flicking raised tail; trilling song

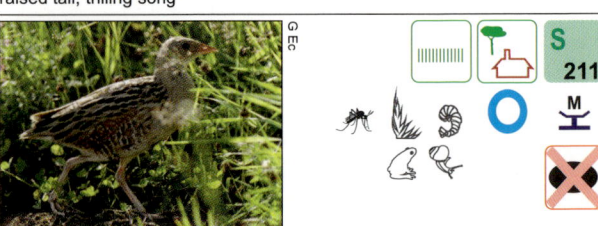

Corn Crake / Kwartelkoning
Buff with brown streaks above; greyish wash on head and breast, short bill, rusty wings, barring on flanks and undertail; secretive

42

S 212

African Crake / Afrikaanse Riethaan
Brown mottled above; red eye, short white eyebrow, grey chest without marks, barring on flanks and belly; crouches when disturbed; active at dusk and dawn

A 213

Black Crake / Swartriethaan

Black with red eyes and yellow-green bill; red legs and feet; flicks tail and jerks head whilst walking; runs fast; call a wheezing duet

A 215

Baillon's Crake / Kleinriethaan

Smallest crake; brown above, grey below; grey face, red eye, dark green bill, white and black flecks on back, bands on flanks, yellow legs; scarce

43

Flufftail

Very small shy and elusive birds, living in thick cover of marshes or the bush. Run fast for cover when disturbed. Females dark and difficult to identify. More often heard than spotted.

A 217

Red-chested Flufftail / Rooiborsvleikuiken
Male rufous head, neck, chest and upper belly; rest of body black with fine white stripes; large hairy black spotted tail, female darker than other flufftail females; inhabits marshy spots

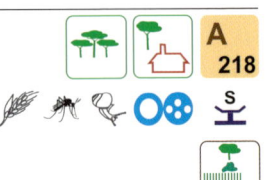

A 218

Buff-spotted Flufftail / Gevlekte Vleikuiken
Male body black with oval golden-buff spots, head and breast chestnut; tail chestnut barred black; voice loud mournful sound mainly heard at night; forest floor species

A 221

Striped Flufftail / Gestreepte Vleikuiken
Mostly blackish-brown with narrow yellowish streaks above and white streaks below; male rufous head and tail, white chin and throat, female rusty head and black barred tail; secretive; forest and grassland

Swamphen, Gallinule, Moorhen & Coot

During the breeding season most have red eyes.

A 223

African Purple Swamphen / Grootkoningriethaan
Deep blue body; greenish back, red shield over red bill, white undertail, big red feet with long thin toes; holds food in feet; often flicks tail

S 224

Fish eggs

Allen's Gallinule / Kleinkoningriethaan
Dark, bluish-green above, dark blue below; dark red bill with blue-green shield, white undertail, red legs; may hold food in feet; shy; inhabits flooded areas

45

Common Moorhen / Grootwaterhoender

Black with white undertail; red eyes, bright red frontal shield, bill red with yellow tip, line of white feathers on flank, green-yellow legs

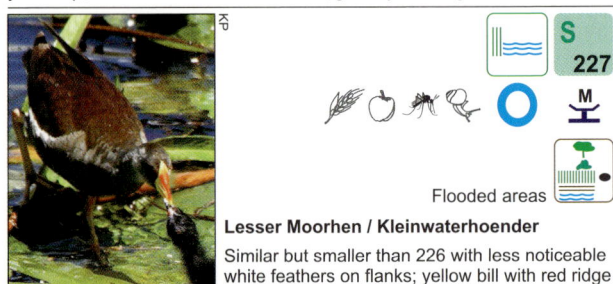

Flooded areas

Lesser Moorhen / Kleinwaterhoender

Similar but smaller than 226 with less noticeable white feathers on flanks; yellow bill with red ridge along the top; secretive

Red-knobbed Coot / Bleshoender

Sooty black; bluish-white bill and forehead shield, two red knobs above shield; floats high on water; mostly swimming, trumpeting and quarrelling

Jacana

Lily-trotters; long legs and toes; walk, breed and feed on floating vegetation; good swimmers; male incubates eggs and cares for the young; carries chicks under his wings.

A 240

African Jacana / Grootlangtoon

Rufous with golden-yellow chest collar; white face, black line through eye, black cap extending to nape, bill and frontal shield pale grey-blue, long slate-grey legs; very vocal

A 241

Restricted distribution

Lesser Jacana / Dwerglangtoon

Rufous-brown above, white below; greenish bill, rufous crown, white eyebrow, black eyestripe, green legs, black underwing in flight; shy; rare

Group 3 — Veld

Crane

Long neck, long black legs; loves to pose, display and dance.

A 209

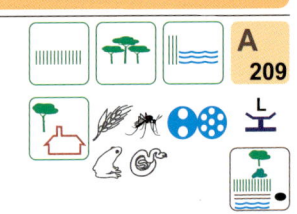

Grey Crowned Crane / Mahem

Mostly grey; black bill, pale blue eyes, head velvety black with bold white cheeks, prominent yellow quills on crown, red wattles, back and neck with dark grey plumes, white upper wing coverts elongated into long loose golden feathering, rufous primaries, black tail; imm. brownish

48

Group 3 – Veld
Dove-like
Dove-shaped birds.

Pigeon
Dove
Sandgrouse

Pigeon

Compact bodies, strong wings, powerful in flight; short bills, thickened at tip, waxy cere over nostrils; often gregarious; nest slight platform of twigs, sticks, feathers and grass.

A ♦
348

D

Rock Dove / Tuinduif
Mostly blue-grey above and light or dark below; neck and upper breast iridescent purple and green, bars on wing, many variations; introduced into South Africa

A
349

D

Speckled Pigeon / Kransduif
Maroon and grey; red patches around eye, wings spotted white; flies long distances to feed, also on cultivated land

49

A 350

Also consumes mud

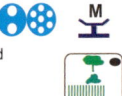

African Olive-Pigeon / Geelbekbosduif

Dark purple-brown spotted white on breast and wings; bill, eye patch and feet yellow, eyes dull yellow, hind crown grey; shy and wary

A 351

Eastern Bronze-naped Pigeon / Withalsbosduif

Overall dark maroon-brown; red eyering, dark legs and feet, male with white collar and mantle; a timid forest canopy bird of evergreen forests; feeds in trees

A 361

Also consumes mud and dry soil

African Green-Pigeon / Papegaaiduif
Yellow-green plumage above, rest soft grey-green; blue eyes, red bill with yellow point, lilac shoulder patch, top of leg yellow feathers, legs red; various sub-species slightly differing in size and colouring

Dove

Generally smaller than pigeons with greyish colour, sometimes tinged purple, blue or rufous. Some have black half-collar on nape. Sexes mostly alike. Feed on ground, compulsive drinkers, highly vocal.

A 352

Red-eyed Dove / Grootringduif

Pinkish tinge to body; pale on top of head, deep red eye and eyering, black half-collar on nape, darker wings, tail grey above, white below

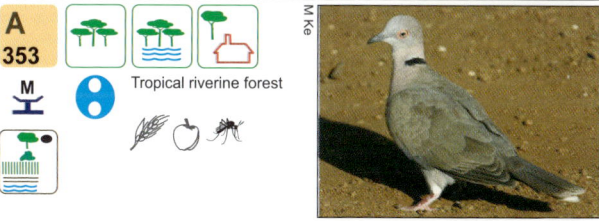

A 353

Tropical riverine forest

African Mourning Dove / Rooioogtortelduif

Grey head, red skin around yellowish eye, black collar on hind-neck, white tail tips, reddish legs and feet

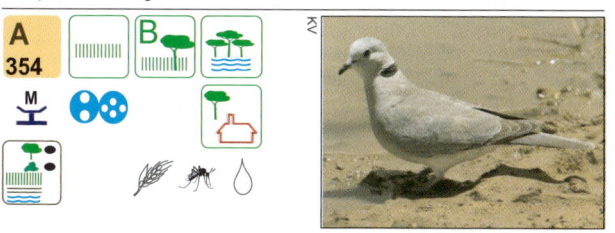

A 354

Cape Turtle-Dove / Gewone Tortelduif

Blue-grey overall; dark eye, half-collar on nape, white-tipped tail seen at take off

51

Laughing Dove / Rooiborsduifie

Soft pink tinge over body; rufous-pink breast speckled black, cinnamon and blue wings, white outertail feathers

Namaqua Dove / Namakwaduifie
Grey above, white below; male black face and throat, maroon and yellow bill, dark and white bands across rump, longish pointed tail, rufous underwing, female without black face, grey bill

Montane evergreen forest

Blue-spotted Wood-Dove / Blouvlekduifie
Light brown above, pinkish-grey below; grey crown, maroon bill with yellow tip, brown eye, iridescent blue patches on wing, rufous on primaries, dark bars on rump; ground loving

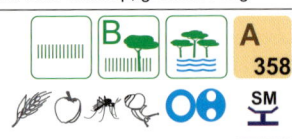

Emerald-spotted Wood-Dove / Groenvlekduifie

Light brown above, pinkish grey below; black bill, grey crown, bands on rump, emerald green spots on wing, rufous underwing; walks with nodding head

A 359

Tambourine Dove / Witborsduifie
Ashy-brown above, white below; white face and eyebrow stripe, bill purplish, two black-purple wing spots, rufous underwings in flight; female grey breast

A 360

Lemon Dove / Kaneelduifie

Dark olive-brown above, cinnamon below; reddish eye with deep pink eyering, black bill, forehead and face whitish, mantle green; ground loving, keeps to dense bush and forest

Sandgrouse

Stocky birds, cryptically coloured; females drab; adapted belly feathers to carry water; short legs; strongly gregarious when flying to water; drink early morning or evening; very vocal. Sexes differ.

A 345

Burchell's Sandgrouse / Gevlekte Sandpatrys
Male reddish ochre, spotted with white; yellow bare skin around eye, lilac-grey chin and throat, female yellowish-buff

53

Double-banded Sandgrouse / Dubbelbandsandpatrys

Male buff with white spotted wings; orange bill, black and white pattern on forehead, yellow eyering, double band on breast

---

Group 3 – Veld
Fowl-like

Fowl-like birds, cryptically coloured, mostly ground-living.

Francolin
Spurfowl
Guineafowl
Quail
Buttonquail

Francolin

Short arched bills with overhanging tips; strong legs and feet for scratching and running; males with one or two spurs; loud call; many roost in trees; shy and wary.

Coqui Francolin / Swempie
Male ochre head and neck, black and white barred belly; only male has spurs; female white eyebrow and white throat bordered by black line; walks very slowly in a stooped manner

54

A 189

Crested Francolin / Bospatrys

Cinnamon brown above; dark cap with crest, often raised, thick white eyebrow, dark spotted and striped chest, red legs; tail sometimes raised; roosts in trees

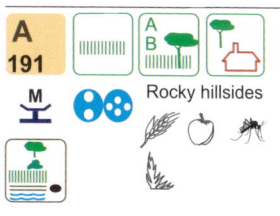

A 191

Rocky hillsides

Shelley's Francolin / Laeveldpatrys

Breast and flanks blotched and striped with chestnut; throat white bordered with black; roosts on ground in coveys

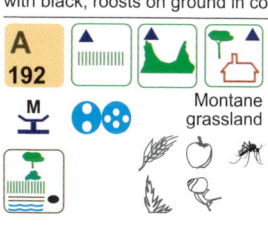

A 192

Montane grassland

Red-winged Francolin / Rooivlerkpatrys

Mottled and streaked brown above, buff below with cinnamon streaked belly; prominent black and white necklace, hindneck tawny-rufous, white throat, rufous wings in flight

A 196

Natal Spurfowl / Natalse Fisant

Dark brown above, black and white feathering below; bill yellow with orange tip, legs orange; roosts in trees; loud excitable call

55

Swainson's Spurfowl / Bosveldfisant
Brown, lighter below streaked with black; bare red eye patch and throat, black legs; calls from tree or other vantage point; roosts in trees

Guinea-fowl

Active terrestrial fowl-like birds occurring in flocks; popular as game birds.

Helmeted Guineafowl / Gewone Tarentaal
Slate with white spots; small bare head with horny helmet, red crown, cere and wattles, light blue around eyes and side of neck; fast runner and strong flier; roosts in trees

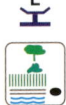

Lowland forest

Crested Guineafowl / Kuifkoptarentaal
Thick crest of curly black feathers; slate black with fine white specks; smallish naked blue head, red eye, white fold of skin from gape to nape, light band on wing; secretive

Quail
Cryptically coloured; highly secretive; call of male usually only indicator of their presence

Buttonquail
Looks like quails but smaller and without a hind toe; male incubates the eggs; somewhat nomadic

A 200

Common Quail / Afrikaanse Kwartel

Small sandy-brown dumpy bird with white and buff streaks; distinct white eyebrow, rounded wings, short tail; runs swiftly; sporadic presence in region

A 201

Harlequin Quail / Bontkwartel

Male brownish streaked white above, chestnut streaked black below; white throat with black breast band, female lighter; calls repeatedly; migrates in flocks; sporadic in region

A 205

Kurrichane Buttonquail / Bosveldkwarteltjie

Straw-coloured; whitish stripe on crown, creamy eyes, pink legs and feet; walks slowly with jerky steps, the body rocking back and forth; female has haunting hooting call

57

Group 3 – Veld
Korhaan-like
Tall birds, long legs.

Bustard
Korhaan
Ostrich

230 Displaying
N St

Bustard
Birds of the open plains, built for running. Long strong legs, stout toes and claws; very wary.

TM MvR

A 230

Gum of thorn trees

Kori Bustard / Gompou
Brown above, belly white; head slightly crested, thick neck, breast finely barred; neck of male inflated in breeding season and during courtship; reluctant flier

TM A Ke

A 238

Black-bellied Bustard / Langbeenkorhaan
Long neck; brown above with black triangular marks; white cheek, thin black line down front neck to black belly, white on wing, female pale, whitish below; secretive

Korhaan

Similar to but smaller than bustards.

A 237

Gum of thorn trees

Red-crested Korhaan / Boskorhaan

Male mottled above, black below; black cap, two white rosettes on chest, red crest only seen when displaying

Ostrich

South Africa's largest bird. A non-flyer. Domesticated and farmed in certain areas.

A 1

Common Ostrich / Volstruis

Long nearly naked neck and legs, large eyes; male mostly black with white-grey or cinnamon curled plumes on the wings and tail, female brownish grey; males may perform elaborate dancing courtship displays; nests up to three metres diameter, clutches of up to 25 eggs laid by several females

Group 3 – Veld

Lapwing-like
Medium birds, long legs.

Thick-knee
Courser
Lapwing

Thick-knee
Cryptic colouring; large head and eyes, stout bill; sexes alike; loud and pleasant call; nocturnal.

A 297

Spotted Thick-knee / Gewone Dikkop

Brown patterned above, spotted below; white eyebrow, large yellow eye, brown streaked breast, yellow legs; squats when disturbed; away from water

A 298

Water Thick-knee / Waterdikkop

Light brown back, white below; black and yellow bill, pale buffy chest, black and white bars above grey primaries, greenish legs

Courser

Large eyes; long legs, short toes, short wings and square tail; normally on dry plains; run with astonishing speed, seldom fly; blend into the environment; easily overlooked.

A 300

Temminck's Courser / Trekdrawwertjie
Rufous crown, white eyebrow and black eyestripe extending to back of neck, chestnut breast, black patch on belly; bobbing movement when alarmed

A 302 Nocturnal

Three-banded Courser / Driebanddrawwertjie
Rich brown to buff above, white below with three black and brown bands, the centre one broad, across the neck and breast; broad white eyebrow ending on nape, yellow bill tipped black; brown upper tail showing white in flight

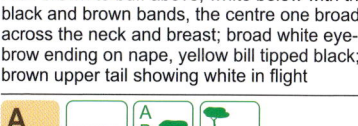

A 303 Nocturnal

Bronze-winged Courser / Bronsvlerkdrawwertjie
Bronze-brown; bold dark brown and white face markings, deep red eyering, red bill tipped black, brown breast band, buff belly, deep red legs

61

Lapwing

All with sharp carpal spurs. Prefer lightly wooded savanna with short grass cover; some species near water.

Crowned Lapwing / Kroonkiewiet

Brown above, white below; black and white banded cap, red bill with black tip, dark breast band, red legs; noisy

Earthworms

Senegal Lapwing / Kleinswartvlerkkiewiet

Greyish-brown above, white below with narrow black breast band; black eyering, small white patch on forehead not touching eyes, white patches on inner wing feathers and tail

62

A 258

Blacksmith Lapwing / Bontkiewiet

Strongly patterned black, white and grey; black legs; very vocal sounding like blacksmith hammering an anvil

A 259

White-crowned Lapwing / Witkopkiewiet

Head and neck grey, brown back, white below; broad white stripe across crown, pale yellow eye, large yellow lappets hanging from yellow and black bill, white wings with black primaries; shy and wary

A 260

African Wattled Lapwing / Lelkiewiet

Greyish-brown; white patch on forehead, cheek wattles yellow, yellow bill with black tip, neck heavily streaked; yellow legs

Group 3 – Veld
LBJ's

Very small, mostly dull brown birds. Plumage and pattern similar. Difficult to identify.

Cisticola
Grassbird
Lark
Pipit

Longclaw
Wagtail
Warbler

Cisticola

Cryptically coloured birds melting into habitat except for some in their breeding plumage. Habitat specific. Distribution and distinctive calls very important identification factors.

Grassveld Cisticolas

Very small short-tailed and closely similar species. Each has a display ritual with distinctive calls and behaviour.

A 664

Zitting Cisticola / Landeryklopkloppie

Tail black and white; prolonged dipping flight, uttering slow "zit-zit-zit" as it drops; flicks tail sideways; prefers damp grassy areas

A 665

Desert Cisticola / Woestynklopkloppie
Pale overall with fairly long tail; snaps wings physically and does much darting and swooping; fast "ting-ting-ting" sound; found in short grass and low basal cover

A 666

Cloud Cisticola / Gevlekte Klopkloppie
Very thickset with short tail; conspicuous long legs; very high aerial display without wing snaps while uttering bold squeaking two-note whistle; often on slopes

A 667

Wing-snapping Cisticola / Kleinste Klopkloppie
Appears slim; very high aerial display with squeaky whistles and wing snapping; prefers short grassland with higher rainfall

Longer-tailed Cisticolas

Wailing Cisticola / Huiltinktinkie

Greyish-brown above with dark brown mottling, warm buff below; rust-red crown, wing with russet bar; inhabits mountainous grassland

Rattling Cisticola / Bosveldtinkie

Russet crown, brown mantle, brown-rufous streaked back, creamy-white below; highly vocal singing from tree tops; voice two high-pitched notes followed by a "cherrrr"

Red-faced Cisticola / Rooiwangtinktinkie

Plain olive-grey above, buff below; rufous face, dark marks on russet-brown tail; mainly along wooded fringes of rivers

66

A 675

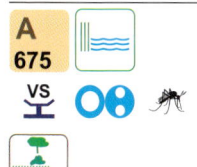

Rufous-winged Cisticola / Swartrugtintinkie

Dull rufous crown, short buff eyebrow, grey mottled black back, grey tail feathers; frequents moist grassland and vlei areas

A 677

Levaillant's Cisticola / Vleitinktinkie

Bright chestnut on the crown, white eyebrow extending behind eye, chestnut back with black feathers edged brown, rufous tail; frequents moist grassland and vlei areas

A 678

Croaking Cisticola / Groottinktinkie

Robust; streaky backed without any rufous tones; black striped crown, heavy bill, grey tail, call a frog-like croak; moist grasslands

A 679

Lazy Cisticola / Luitinktinkie

Rufous crown, plain-looking back, warm-buffy below; unusually long tail often cocked like that of a prinia; no aerial display (hence the name); frequents rocky hilly areas; can be confused with prinias

Neddicky / Neddikkie
Very small; red-brown crown, plain back, buffy-grey below; perches high in trees wagging short tail sideways; always associated with trees and bushes; forages on ground and in undergrowth

Grassbird
Shaggy appearance, sexes alike.

Cape Grassbird / Grasvoël
Buff with black streaks; bright rufous head well marked with two black malar stripes, longish untidy tail; reluctant flier; creeps through undergrowth

Lark

Cryptically coloured, melting into habitat. White or buff outertail feathers. Longish toes, well-developed hindclaws; sexes alike; wonderful flight display. Two distinct habitat preferences in group.

Woodland Larks

Species found in woodland areas including grassland with scattered bushes and open woodland.

A 493

Monotonous Lark / Bosveldlewerik

Streaky-brown crown, short stout bill, rufous on the wings; sings day and night from a perch with a white puffed throat; nomadic

A 494

Rufous-naped Lark / Rooineklewerik

Chunky bird; bright rufous primaries, buff-rufous below; sings from perch; will raise crest and do wing rattle

69

Flappet Lark / Laeveldklappertjie

Scaly-like markings on the wing as well as a rufous panel; sometimes with erect crest; shy except when male is displaying

Fawn-coloured Lark / Vaalbruinlewerik

Buff-rufous above, white below; white eyebrow, rufous ear coverts, straight line between head and neck, lightly streaked breast, squarish tail; prefers sandy soil areas; rare

Sabota Lark / Sabotalewerik

Distinctive striped head pattern, white eyebrow, black stripe through eye, clearly marked breast, buff-white below; crouches when walking; mimics other bird calls

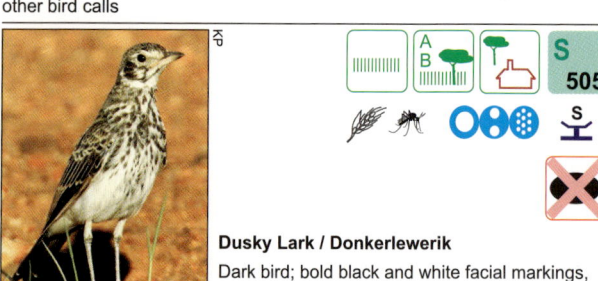

Dusky Lark / Donkerlewerik

Dark bird; bold black and white facial markings, heavily streaked white breast; upright stance; perches in trees; will raise wings when walking

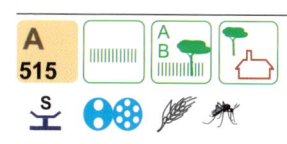

Chestnut-backed Sparrowlark / Rooiruglewerik

Chestnut back, black below; male head black with large white ear patch and narrow whitish collar on nape, female chestnut back, white below with black patch on the belly, pale collar; rarely perches; nomadic

Open veld Larks

Species found in open veld including grassveld, sandveld and shrubby areas.

Eastern Long-billed Lark / Grasveldlangbeklewerik

Red-brown above, buff below lightly streaked; clear white eyebrow, long decurved bill, longish tail; descending "pooooeeee" sound; rocky ridges

Red-capped Lark / Rooikoplewerik

Brown above, whitish below; chestnut cap, rufous patches on the side of the chest, square tail; raises crest when excited or hot; nomadic

71

Grey-backed Sparrowlark / Grysruglewerik
Drab grey above, black below; blue-grey bill, male black head with white ear patches, white patch on hindcrown, female greyer; nomadic

Pipit

Nondescript and dull. Most with crown stripes and white or buffy outertail feathers; fairly long-legged. Mainly ground dwellers in grassy habitat. Most males have aerial or injury-feigning displays.

Marked-backed Pipits

Two species distinctly streaked on back and breast.

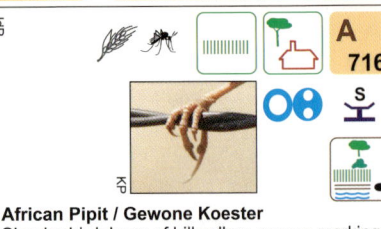

African Pipit / Gewone Koester
Slender bird; base of bill yellow, narrow markings on buffy breast, pure white outertail feathers; dips tail one to three times at each stop; dipping display flight; common

A 717

Long-billed Pipit / Nicholsonse Koester

Mostly a pale sandy colour; large thick bill with yellow base, upper breast streaked; two- to three-note call; prefers rocky grassland slopes

Plain-backed Pipits

Two species; no markings on the back and buffy below with indistinct breast markings. Prefer short grassland or over-grazed areas.

A 718

Plain-backed Pipit / Donkerkoester

Dark above; bill with yellowish base, eyebrow buffy white, longish dark tail; downward tail wagging; posture not boldly upright; prominent two-note call

A 719

Buffy Pipit / Vaalkoester

Buff coloured; pink base on bill, buffy eyebrow, stands very erect; frequently wags tail; found in low-lying savanna areas; nomadic

Boldly streaked Pipits

Three species with bold streaking on the breast.

Striped Pipit / Gestreepte Koester
Buffy-olive above, white below boldly and closely streaked dark brown; bright yellow on the wing, tail and outertail feathers; prefers rocky woodland areas and steep slopes

Tree Pipit / Boomkoester
Yellow-green above, black malar stripe, very white chin, strong brown markings on breast, slight streaking on flanks, white outertail feathers; walks in crouched position; wags tail when pausing; forest edge bird; high-pitched nasal call; uncommon

Bushveld Pipit / Bosveldkoester
Smallest pipit; buffy; bold streaking on breast, short tail with white outertail feathers; forages in crouched position; wary and will fly into trees when disturbed; nomadic

Longclaw

Brightly coloured, prominent black necklace, extremely long hindclaws; fly with white-tipped tail spread.

A 727

Cape Longclaw / Oranjekeelkalkoentjie
Spotted and streaked brown above, ochre yellow below; eyebrow yellow, throat bright orange with black collar; partial to damp areas; mewing call

A 728

Yellow-throated Longclaw / Geelkeelkalkoentjie
Buffy-brown above, bright yellow below vaguely streaked; broad black necklace across upper breast, white-tipped outertail feathers; loud drawn-out call

75

Wagtail

Long to very long tails and white outertail feathers. Wag tails in bobbing movement.

A 711

African Pied Wagtail / Bontkwikkie
Conspicuous black and white bird; white eyebrow, chin and patch on side of neck, black breast band, broad white wing stripe, white below; female more brownish

A 712

Flowing streams

Stream banks

Mountain Wagtail / Bergkwikkie
Blue-grey above, white below; thin black breast band, wings with black and white markings, unusually long tail; feeds on wet rocks near fast-flowing streams and waterfalls

A 713

Cape Wagtail / Gewone Kwikkie
Grey above without markings, dull buff below with a grey wash; slight eyebrow, black breast band; wags tail all the time; cheerful

S 714

Yellow Wagtail / Geelkwikkie
Olive above, yellowish below; thin eyestripe, shortish tail, variable plumage, head colour differs between races; more upright stance and less tail wagging than rest of group

S 715

Grey Wagtail / Gryskwikkie
Grey above, yellow below; narrow white eyestripe, white malar stripe, yellow-green rump, white flanks, pink legs, black throat and upper breast when breeding; rare

Warbler

Sloping foreheads, plain plumage, sexes alike; skulking behaviour. Identified by combination of factors such as plumage, voice and habitat.

S 609

Thrush Nightingale / Lysternagtegaal
Brown above shading to rufous on wing tips, rump and tail, dull white below; breast and flanks slightly mottled; extremely timid and skulking; sings well; arrives late in season

77

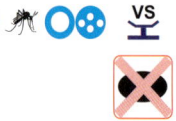

Garden Warbler / Tuinsanger

Plump, drab grey-brown above, paler below; rounded head, slight eyebrow, short bill; sings from concealed position deep in bush

Common Whitethroat / Witkeelsanger

Male grey head and white throat, reddish-brown panel in the wings, female brown head, tail brown with white outertail feathers, pinkish-grey below; usually skulks; crown feathers raised when excited

Icterine Warbler / Spotsanger

Olive-grey above, lemon-yellow below; yellow lower mandible, pale yellow eyebrow, yellow panel in wing; flicks short tail; restless

Olive-tree Warbler / Olyfboomsanger

Greyish warbler; long heavy bill, short white eyebrow stretching from bill to eyebrow, narrow white eyering, lighter outertail feathers; skulking; forages in thick cover

S 627

River Warbler / Sprinkaansanger
Brownish above and buff below, streaked brown on lower throat and breast; graduated rounded tail with broad white tips on undertail; unobtrusive

S 628

Great Reed-Warbler / Grootrietsanger
Largest warbler, robust; olive-brown above, lighter below; long bill, buff eyebrow stripe; located by harsh croaking call; sometimes far from water

A 631

African Reed-Warbler / Kleinrietsanger
Smallest of reed warblers; brown with red-brown tinge above, buff below; long fine bill, short wing ending on rufous rump, rufous tail; mainly found in reed beds

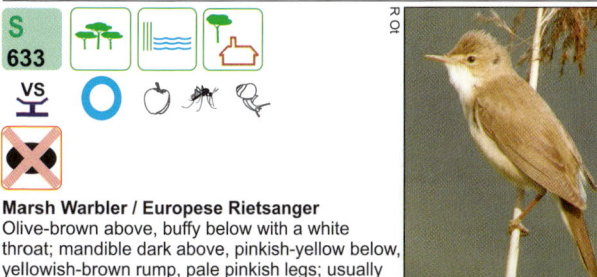

S 633

Marsh Warbler / Europese Rietsanger
Olive-brown above, buffy below with a white throat; mandible dark above, pinkish-yellow below, yellowish-brown rump, pale pinkish legs; usually found in drier areas and often far from water

79

Sedge Warbler / Europese Vleisanger

Olive-brown above, buff below; only warbler with black streaked crown, broad creamy-white eyebrow; sometimes found far from water

Lesser Swamp-Warbler / Kaapse Rietsanger

Robust; rufous-brown; white or creamy eyebrow, more white below than other species; highly vocal; always associated with reed beds

Dark-capped Yellow Warbler / Geelsanger

Olive-brown to red-brown above, bright yellow below; broad flat bill, yellow rump; sings well; hawks like a flycatcher

Little Rush-Warbler / Kaapse Vleisanger

Very dark smokey-brown; buffy-white eyebrow, rufous overlay on rump and rounded tail, outertail feathers barred black; tail spread in flight; shy; distinctive call

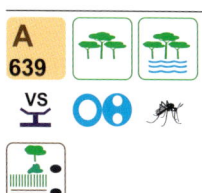

Barratt's Warbler / Ruigtesanger

Rich dark brown above, greyish-white below; faintly streaked on throat and breast, chestnut overlay on rump and rounded tail; keeps near the ground, seldom in reed beds

Broad-tailed Warbler / Breëstertsanger

Greyish-brown above, buff below; flattened forehead, long broad black tail with buff markings underneath

Willow Warbler / Hofsanger

Slender; yellow-brown above, soft yellow below; thin bill, pale yellow or white eyebrow; usually heard before seen

81

Group 4 – Birds of Prey

Eagle-like

Large raptors, hooked beaks, strong talons.

Secretarybird
Kite
Allied species
Eagle

Snake-Eagle
Fish-eating raptors
Buzzard

Secretary-bird

Raptor-like; adapted to live on ground; name originates from Arabic "saqr-et-tair" meaning hunter bird.

A 118

Secretarybird / Sekretarisvoël
Mainly pale grey and black; black plumes on crown, bare orange facial skin (red when breeding and yellow in juvenile), long tail with black band, long pinkish legs; strong padded toes

Kite

Scavengers perching on fences and telephone or power lines; frequently use road kills as a food source; also eat smaller animals.

S 126

Black Kite / Swartwou
Brown; grey head, black beak with yellow cere, pale eye, rufous brown breast with dark stripes, long wings, squarish slightly forked tail, shortish yellow bare legs; mostly silent in South Africa; scarce

A 126.1 (940)

Yellow-billed Kite / Geelbekwou
Uniform brown; brown eye, yellow beak and cere, long forked tail, yellow legs and feet, juv. rufous feathers on legs; very adaptable; opportunistic

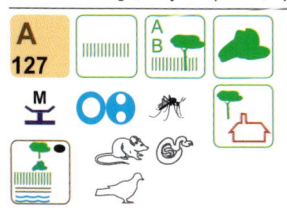

A 127

Black-shouldered Kite / Blouvalk
Grey above, white below; red eye, black beak and yellow cere, long wings with black shoulder patches, yellow legs; hovers when hunting

83

Allied species

African Cuckoo Hawk / Koekoekvalk
Dark grey above; breast grey, belly and underwing white to buff with broad rufous bars, slight crest at back of neck, male wine red eye, female yellow eye, pointed wings, long banded tail, short yellow legs

Bat Hawk / Vlermuisvalk
Short hind crest, long pointed wings, longish tail; mostly dark brown, varying white below; yellow eyes, white eyelids, false eye patches on nape, white throat with vertical black stripe, white bare legs

Bats

Wasp larvae and pupae

European Honey-Buzzard / Wespedief
Slim; variably coloured; small pigeon-like head; large yellow eyes; long tail; thick feathers on face and scales on short legs for protection against wasps

Eagle

Large birds with powerful hooked beaks, unusually strong yellow talons and completely feathered legs. Normally long and broad wings.

Large Eagles

A 131

Verreauxs' Eagle / Witkruisarend

Jet-black; yellow eyelids, cere and gape, white V on back, yellow legs and feet, white rump, pale windows in primaries visible in flight

A 140

Martial Eagle / Breëkoparend

Largest eagle; dark brown above, white below with dark brown spotting; flat broad head with crest, large black beak, yellow eye

85

African Crowned Eagle / Kroonarend
Crest on head, long tail; dark slaty red-brown above, rufous below with heavy black and white mottling; yellow eye, gape and feet, heavily barred tail

Brown Eagles

Tawny Eagle / Roofarend

Termites

Colour variable from creamy to tawny and dark brown; gape extends to line level with the middle of the eye, baggy feathering on legs

Steppe Eagle / Steppe-arend

Termites & quelea chicks

Chocolate brown colour; large yellow-orange gape that extends to back of eye, banded tail, baggy leggings, yellow feet

86

S 134

Termites & quelea chicks

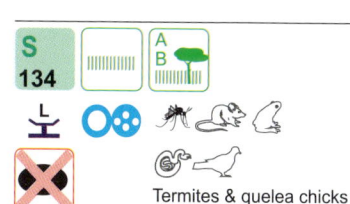

Lesser Spotted Eagle / Gevlekte Arend
Dark brown; short neck, yellow eye (juvenile brown), short and rounded tail, narrow tightly feathered legs, white rump in flight; immature more common in SA

A 135

Bats

Wahlberg's Eagle / Bruinarend
Slimly built; usually dark brown but variable to beige; sometimes small crest, large gape, narrow wings and slim rectangular tail

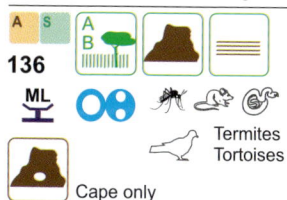

A S 136

Termites
Tortoises

Cape only

Booted Eagle / Dwergarend
Smallest SA eagle; dark brown above, beige or white below; brown head, soft streaking on breast and flanks, heavily feathered legs

A 139

Long-crested Eagle / Langkuifarend
Blackish-brown; long wavy crest, yellow eyes and yellow gape, males have white leg feathering; shows white "landing lights" on underwing

Hawk-Eagle

African Hawk-Eagle / Grootjagarend
Dark above, white below with black streaks; yellow eye, pale barred tail with broad black terminal band, white underwing with broad black trailing edge, immature brown above, rufous below and slightly streaked with brown eyes

Bats

Ayres's Hawk-Eagle / Kleinjagarend
Very dark above, white below with heavy black blotching also on legs and underwing; small crest, white patch on shoulder of wing; tail heavily barred; rare; forest species; easily overlooked

Snake-Eagle

Medium to large sized raptors with a bold upright posture; large heads; most have big yellow owl-like eyes; long broad wings; naked scaly legs; strong short claws.

A 142

Brown Snake-Eagle / Bruinslangarend

Dark brown; black beak, greyish-white cere, tail barred, greyish-white legs, white flight feathers, immature with white mottling on belly

A 143

Black-chested Snake-Eagle / Swartborsslangarend

Black all over except for white lower breast and belly; legs and feet white, shows white underwing in flight, imm. brownish with barring on flanks

A 146

Bateleur / Berghaan

Large head; mainly black; red beak tipped yellow, red cere and bare facial skin, brown eye, chestnut mantle and back, long wings with upswept tips, short chestnut tail, red legs, female white flight feathers

89

Fish-eating Raptors

No feathering on lower legs.

African Fish-Eagle / Visarend

Dark brown; white head, neck and breast; yellow beak tipped black, cere and lores yellow, short white tail, naked yellow legs

Osprey / Visvalk

Brown above, white below; small head, white crown, brown line through yellow eye, long barred tail, naked blue-grey legs and claws

Buzzard

Smaller than eagles with shorter wings and only upper leg feathering; medium to shortish tails held widespread in flight; mature birds have dark eyes, immature light eyes.

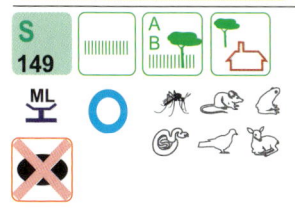

149 Juv.

S 149

Steppe Buzzard / Bruinjakkalsvoël

Brown above, brown blotched or barred below; yellow cere, brown eye, chestnut band across chest, yellow legs and feet; much variation

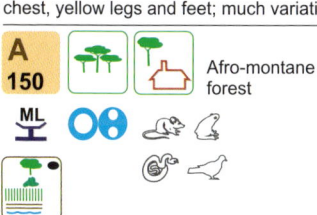

A 150

Afro-montane forest

Forest Buzzard / Bosjakkalsvoël

Brown above, pale below with blotches (not bars); variable; light brown eye; sometimes white band across breast; rare; local

A 152

Jackal Buzzard / Rooiborsjakkalsvoël

Broad shoulders; dark grey-black above, rufous chest, black belly with white barring, distinctive black-and-white underwing, rufous tail; also see page 1

91

Group 4 – Birds of Prey
Falcon-like
Smaller raptors.

Goshawk
Sparrowhawk
Harrier-Hawk

Harrier
Falcon
Kestrel

Goshawk and Sparrowhawk

Small to medium slender-bodied birds; short and rounded wings; long legs and tails; mostly grey with different patterns of barring; females larger than males.

A 154

Lizard Buzzard / Akkedisvalk

Dark grey above, grey breast, belly finely barred; pink cere, red eye, white throat with black vertical stripe, white rump, red legs

Afro-montane forest

A 155

Rufous-chested Sparrowhawk / Rooiborssperwer

Slate above, plain rufous below; head slate-grey to below the yellow eye, underwing and tail banded; hunts in open areas

A 156

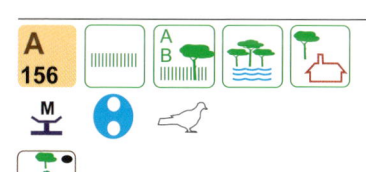

Ovambo Sparrowhawk / Ovambosperwer

Small head; dark grey above, banded below; wine-red eye, red-orange cere and gape, grey rump, red legs; also melanistic form

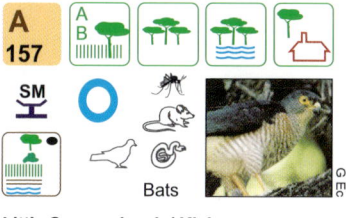

A 157

Bats

Little Sparrowhawk / Kleinsperwer

Smallest of group; grey above, white below barred rufous-brown; black beak, yellow cere and eye, uppertail with two central eyespots, legs yellow

A 158

Bats

Black Sparrowhawk / Swartsperwer

Black above, white below; cere yellow, eye wine-red, banded tail, yellow legs, melanistic form sometimes has white mark on throat

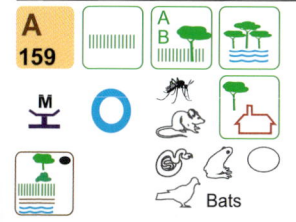

A 159

Bats

Shrika / Gebande Sperwer

Grey above, white below barred grey, female barred rufous; yellow cere, cherry-red eye, female orange eye, grey rump, dark tail, yellow legs; vocal

93

African Goshawk / Afrikaanse Sperwer
Male slate above and white with narrow russet bars in front; yellow eye, long barred tail, yellow legs; female larger, brown and barred in front

Gabar Goshawk / Witkruissperwer (Kleinsingvalk)
Dark grey above, smooth grey on throat and upper breast, finely barred below; red cere, brown-red eye, white rump, barred tail, red legs; sexes alike; also melanistic form

Chanting Goshawk

Bigger than true goshawks; medium to large with characteristic build; roadside birds; hunt on the ground; prefer semi-arid to open savanna areas.

A 162

Southern Pale Chanting Goshawk / Bleeksingvalk
Grey above, upper breast light grey, belly finely barred grey; red cere, dark eye, black tips on underwings, broad white rump, long orange legs

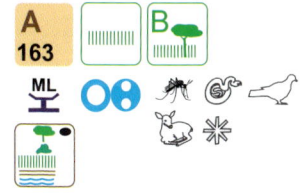

A 163

Dark Chanting Goshawk / Donkersingvalk
Dark grey above, dark grey on upper breast, whitish with fine grey barring below; red cere and legs, grey underwing with black tip, barred rump

95

Harrier-Hawk (Gymnogene)

Skin on face red when displaying or alarmed.

African Harrier-Hawk / Kaalwangvalk
Small head; dark grey above, grey breast, black barred belly; yellow cere and bare facial skin; black tail with white bar across, long yellow legs

Marsh-Harrier

Slender bodies, yellow eyes, suggestion of a facial disc; long yellow naked legs; long wings and tails; frequently glide; difficult to distinguish between the female marsh harriers.

Western Marsh-Harrier / Europese Vleivalk (Europese Paddavreter)
Dark brown above, dull rufous below; male grey head and wing shoulder, black wing tips, unmarked grey tail, female chocolate brown with almost white crown, chin and wing shoulder, unmarked brown tail

96

A 165

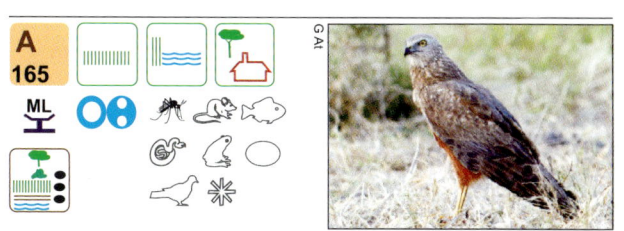

African Marsh-Harrier / Afrikaanse Vleivalk (Afrikaanse Paddavreter)
Brown bird with light stripes on head, neck, back and flanks, long banded tail, rufous belly and leggings; female darker than male, immature with pale breast bar

S 166

Montagu's Harrier / Blouvleivalk (Bloupaddavreter)
Male dark grey above, white below with streaks on belly and flanks; grey throat and upper breast, wing with black wing bar and wing tip, underwing streaked rufous, black tip; female brownish

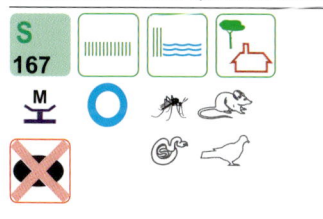

S 167

Pallid Harrier / Witborsvleivalk (Witborspaddavreter)
Male grey above, light grey below; grey head and chest, underwing white with small black tip; female brownish with small white rump and banded tail

97

True Falcons

Small to medium streamlined bodies, long tails, pointed wings; dark eyes; some with dark malar stripes; most have yellow ceres, eyerings and legs.

Peregrine Falcon / Swerfvalk
Dark grey-black above, light below spotted on the chest and finely barred on the belly; black head, banded underwing; scarce

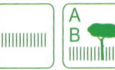

Lanner Falcon / Edelvalk
Brown-grey above, plain pinkish or whitish below; rufous head, prominent malar stripes, banded underwing; imm. dark brown above and lighter below

Eurasian Hobby / Europese Boomvalk
Slender; dark grey above, heavily streaked underparts; heavy malar stripes, rufous lower belly and leg feathers, immature brown above and lighter below

98

S 174

African Hobby / Afrikaanse Boomvalk

Slaty black above, completely rufous below; blackish crown and malar stripes, yellow cere, eyering and feet, underwing rufous; dusk and dawn hunter; rare

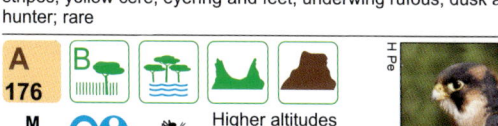

A 176

Higher altitudes

Taita Falcon / Taitavalk

Similar to 174 but more robust, whitish cheeks and throat, rufous patches on nape; rare; local; seldom seen in veld

Red-footed Falcon

Very agile; virtually only difference in males is in colour of underwing coverts; mostly occur in large groups.

S 179

Red-footed Falcon / Westelike Rooipootvalk

Male dark slate-grey above, paler blue-grey below; orange cere, eyering, legs and feet, rufous underbelly and upper legs; female dark above barred black, rufous below; rufous head, mottled underwing coverts and tail

99

Amur Falcon / Oostelike Rooipootvalk

Male slate above, paler blue-grey below; white underwing coverts. Female blue-grey above, white with heavy black streaks below, prominent malar stripe. In both sexes cere, eyering, legs and feet orange to orange-red, lower belly light chestnut

Kestrel

Red-brown birds mostly hovering along roadsides; adult birds have yellow cere, legs and feet; will also hunt from perch.

Bats

Rock Kestrel / Kransvalk

Grey head with dark stripes, speckled rufous back and chest; banded white underwing, grey tail with white point and broad subterminal band

Greater Kestrel / Grootrooivalk

Rufous with barring across back, striped underparts; eye pale yellow to white, underwing mostly white, tail grey with dark bands; sexes alike

Lesser Kestrel / Kleinrooivalk

Reddish-brown above, pale brown below; blue-grey head, wing and tail, band across tail, female pale whitish to reddish brown, dark blotches on back, streaked below

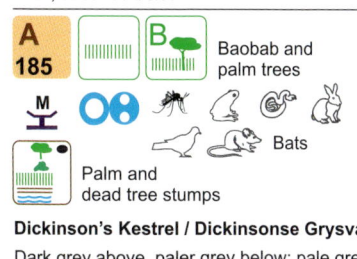

Baobab and palm trees

Palm and dead tree stumps

Dickinson's Kestrel / Dickinsonse Grysvalk

Dark grey above, paler grey below; pale grey square-shaped head, yellow cere, eyering and legs, white rump, barred tail; rare

101

Group 4 – Birds of Prey

Owl

Nocturnal birds cryptically coloured in grey, buff, brown or white; large heads, flattened facial discs, large forward looking eyes, short hooked beaks, short necks, long feathered legs, long curved talons; silent flyers; regurgitate pellets of undigested parts of prey; all have characteristic calls.

Barn Owl / Nonnetjie-uil
Slender body, large head; pale beak, heart-shaped facial disc, dark eyes, warm orange-brown back and wings, underwing white, short barred tail

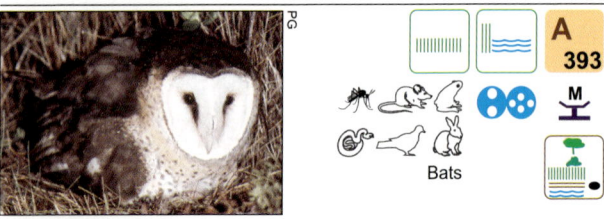

African Grass-Owl / Grasuil
Slender body; dark brown above, buffy-brown below with half-moon spots; pale beak, white heart-shaped facial disc, dark eyes, almost black underwing, short white tail; lands directly in grass

A 394

African Wood-Owl / Bosuil
Dark brown to red-brown above, whitish below, completely barred with chestnut and buff; no ear tufts; white face with brown around the dark eye, yellow beak, white spots on wings, longish barred tail

A 395

Marsh Owl / Vlei-uil
Brown; black beak, small ear tufts not normally shown, dark marks around dark brown eyes, buff-brown barred tail

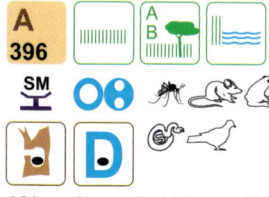

A 396

African Scops-Owl / Skopsuil
Grey, streaked black and brown; black beak, elongated ear tufts, grey facial disc with black border, bright yellow eyes, short tail; also brown form

A 397

Southern White-faced Scops-Owl / Witwanguil
Pale grey above streaked black, white below streaked black; prominent ear tufts, pale white facial disc with black border, long white bristles around beak, orange eyes

103

Pearl-spotted Owlet / Witkoluil
A 398

Big head, no ear tufts; brown above with white spots and streaks, white below broadly streaked brown; pale green to yellow beak, bright yellow eyes, false eyes behind head

African Barred Owlet / Gebande Uil
A 399

No ear tufts; brown banded above, white below barred and spotted brown; roundish barred head, yellow eyes, white eyebrows, white V on back

Cape Eagle-Owl / Kaapse Ooruil
A 400

Dark spotted above, bold brown and rufous blotching on chest, heavy barring on whitish belly; prominent ear tufts, orange eyes, large feet, very strong talons; scarce

Spotted Eagle-Owl / Gevlekte Ooruil
A 401

Grey-brown; blotched above, finely barred below; black beak, prominent ear tufts, bright yellow eyes

104

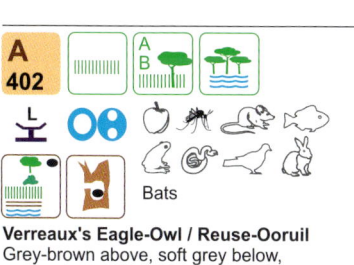

A 402

Verreaux's Eagle-Owl / Reuse-Ooruil
Grey-brown above, soft grey below, vermiculated; pink beak; prominent ear tufts, facial disc with black outer rim, dark brown eyes, conspicuous pink eyelids

A 403

Bats

Pel's Fishing-Owl / Visuil
Tawny-rufous above with brown barring, tawny-buff below with brown spots; dark eyes, no ear tufts but can fluff up crown feathers; rare; vulnerable

400

105

Group 5 – Scavengers
Vulture

Nearly bare heads and necks; powerful hooked beaks; long broad wings and short tails; strong talons; sexes alike; soar magnificently.

A 121

Hooded Vulture / Monnikaasvoël

Mostly blackish brown; slender black beak, pink bare head and front neck, short white down on hindneck, dark underwing, white leggings

A 122

Cape Vulture / Kransaasvoël

Plain buffy brown; bluish bare facial skin; light eye, bare blue patches on either side of the base of the neck, black wing tips and tail

A 123

White-backed Vulture / Witrugaasvoël

Brown; blackish facial skin; dark eye, pinkish neck with whitish feathering, only mature adults over six years have white backs

A 124

Lappet-faced Vulture / Swartaasvoël
Brown above, white below with streaking on breast; red and blue head and neck with lappets of skin, big yellowish beak, white leg feathers

A 125

White-headed Vulture / Witkopaasvoël
Black above and on breast, white belly; white triangular-shaped head, amber eye, light blue beak with pink front end, pink facial skin, black collar at base of neck, white leggings

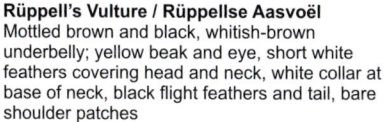

S 933 Vagrant

Rüppell's Vulture / Rüppellse Aasvoël
Mottled brown and black, whitish-brown underbelly; yellow beak and eye, short white feathers covering head and neck, white collar at base of neck, black flight feathers and tail, bare shoulder patches

107

Group 6 – Nectar feeders

Sunbird-like

Small birds, slender curved bills.

Sugarbird
Sunbird

Sugarbird

Resemble sunbirds but larger and more sombre colouring; long tail, that of female shorter; often sit with tail blowing in the wind; mainly nectar feeders; frequent protea and aloe habitat.

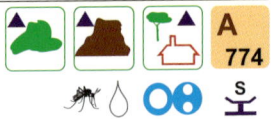

A 774

Gurney's Sugarbird / Rooiborssuikervoël

Rufous on the crown, throat and breast, belly white; bright yellow under the long tail; fast flier with tail streaming out from behind; sexes alike

Sunbird

Small metallic coloured birds with long bills for probing flowers; females drab; hover to catch insects or spiders on their webs; most males display bright pectoral feathers in the shoulder when breeding or with aggressive behaviour.

A 775

Malachite Sunbird / Jangroentjie

Malachite green except on the primaries and the long tail, which are blue-black; male pectoral feathers yellow, female brown above, soft yellow below; sometimes nests over a stream

A 779

Marico Sunbird / Maricosuikerbekkie

Metallic green above shading to blue-green on the rump, black below; blue and purple-maroon breast bands

109

Purple-banded Sunbird / Purperbandsuikerbekkie

Smaller and shorter billed than 779; metallic green upperparts and breast, black lower belly; purple-maroon breast band, blue rump.

Southern Double-collared Sunbird / Kleinrooibandsuikerbekkie

Similar but smaller, shorter-billed and narrower red breast band than 785; yellow pectoral feathers, greyish belly, blue rump

Greater Double-collared Sunbird / Grootrooibandsuikerbekkie

Head, throat and back metallic green, rump blue-green, broad red breast band, pectoral feathers yellow; often hovers

White-bellied Sunbird / Witpenssuikerbekkie

Metallic green above, white below; head metallic green, blue breast band, pectoral feathers lemon-yellow; highly vocal

110

A 791

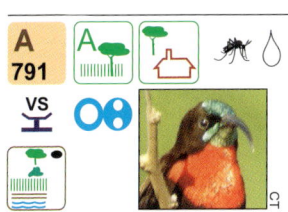

Scarlet-chested Sunbird / Rooiborssuikerbekkie

Mostly black except for the vivid scarlet chest; forehead and throat iridescent green; no pectoral feathers

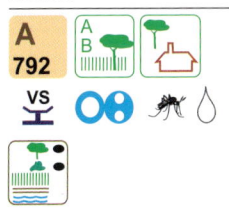

A 792

Amethyst Sunbird / Swartsuikerbekkie

Male velvety purple-black with a metallic green patch on the head and a metallic purple throat

A 793

Collared Sunbird / Kortbekbsuikerbekkie

Short bill; glossy green upperparts and head, bright yellow below; narrow purple breast band, lemon-yellow pectoral feathers; mostly insect eater

111

Group 7 – Unusual feeders
Adapted bills
Fairly heavy strong specially adapted bills.

Coucal
Crow and Raven
Oxpecker
Honeyguide

Coucal
Short rounded wings and broad tails; long strong legs; skulkers flying from cover to cover; run well; love sunning themselves.

A 388

Black Coucal / Swartvleiloerie

Black all over except for chestnut upper back and wings; brown eyes, female larger than male; male undertakes parental care; secretive; rare

A 390

Senegal Coucal / Senegalvleiloerie

Black above, white below; black on head to just below the red eye, chestnut wings, no barring on rump or uppertail

A 391

Burchell's Coucal / Gewone Vleiloerie

Blue-black above, buff below; white chin and throat, chestnut wings, fine rufous barring on rump, long broad tail; creeps through vegetation

Crow

Black, some with white; large strong bills; carrion eaters and cleaners of the environment; frequently eat off the road; common city dwellers.

A 547

Omnivorous

Cape Crow / Swartkraai

Slender slightly decurved bill; glossy black; imm. browner than adults; walks with long strides; small colony in northern region

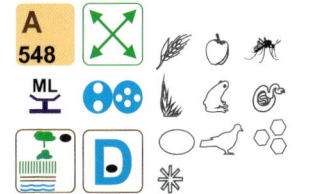

A 548

Pied Crow / Witborskraai

Heavy head; shiny black; heavy black bill, white breast and white collar on hindneck; loud, noisy and bold; largely a scavenger

113

White-necked Raven / Withalskraai

Fairly small head, broad wings; black except for white collar on hindneck, huge black bill with white tip

Oxpecker

Adapted beaks to comb animal fur; short legs and sharp claws for clinging to animals to collect parasites, ticks, mites and body flies; prop themselves with stiff bristle-like tails.

Blood

Yellow-billed Oxpecker / Geelbekrenostervoël

Similar to 772 but a yellow bill with a red tip, red eye, no yellow skin around eye, pale rump; rare and vulnerable

Blood

Red-billed Oxpecker / Rooibekrenostervoël

Dark brown above, buff below; conspicuous red bill; bright yellow skin around the red eye; brown chin and throat; hissing sound warning animals

Honeyguide

Mostly grey to white and grey with white outertail feathers; rare and unique habit of eating wax; breeding parasite.

A 474

Bank & hole nesters

Greater Honeyguide / Grootheuningwyser

Bulky; greyish; pink stubby bill, white ear patches, black throat, yellow on wrist of shoulder; believed to guide humans and animals to bees' nests

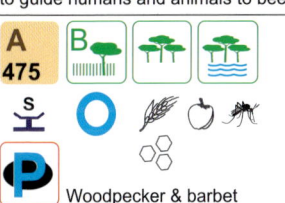

A 475

Woodpecker & barbet

Scaly-throated Honeyguide / Gevlekte Heuningwyser

Olive-grey above, buffy white below; speckled on crown and throat, scaly mottled breast, blackish tail, very shy

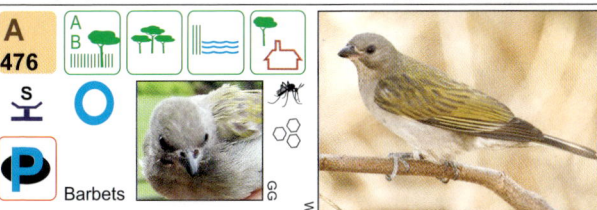

A 476

Barbets

Lesser Honeyguide / Kleinheuningwyser

Dull bird; greenish wash on wings, stubby bill with large nostrils, dark malar stripes, dusky breast, grey rump; crouches on branches

115

Brown-backed Honeybird / Skerpbekheuningvoël
Brown above, grey on breast; slender pointed bill, lighter throat and rump; bobs head sideways; hawks like a flycatcher

Cisticolas

Group 8 — Seed eaters
Sparrow-like
Short conical bills.

Bunting
Canary
Sparrow

Bunting

Golden-breasted Bunting / Rooirugstreepkoppie

Chestnut above with white wing bars, yellow to orange below; black head with white stripes above and under the eye, white outertail feathers

Flower buds

116

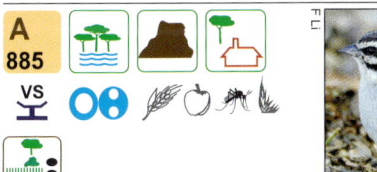

Cape Bunting / Rooivlerkstreepkoppie
Mostly greyish; head striped black and white, white chin, rufous wings; often crouches and turns around after landing; sometimes opens and closes wings when singing

Cinnamon-breasted Bunting / Klipstreepkoppie
Mostly cinnamon; head striped black and white, black throat; reluctant flyer; loves dongas and eroded areas

Lark-like Bunting / Vaalstreepkoppie
Buffy body; pale eyebrow and chin, soft rufous panel on the wing and outertail; nomadic

Canary

Mostly yellow, green or greyish; excellent singers.

A 869

Yellow-fronted Canary / Geeloogkanarie
Greyish above, bright yellow below; grey crown and nape, clear yellow eyebrow stretching across bill, black malar and eyestripe, white tail tip

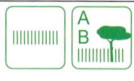

A 870

Acacia gum

Black-throated Canary / Bergkanarie
Drab; finely streaked head and black-speckled throat (not always visible), yellow rump, tail tipped and edged white

Lala palm areas

A 871

Palm fronds

Lemon-breasted Canary / Geelborskanarie
Grey streaked black above, white below; streaky crown, white forecrown, white or yellow cheek patch, noticeable malar stripe, yellow throat and breast, yellow rump, female with buffy throat; scarce; nomadic

A 872

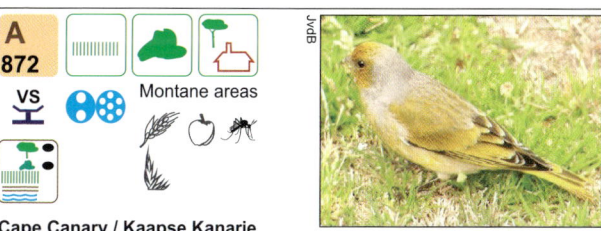

Montane areas

Cape Canary / Kaapse Kanarie

Dull greenish-yellow except for silver-grey on hindneck and mantle; greenish-yellow face and chin, female duller with streaked mantle and blue-grey collar; excellent singer; nomadic

A 873

Forest Canary / Gestreepte Kanarie

Dull olive; heavily streaked nape, back and sides of chest, dark face, short yellow eyestripe, olive-green cheeks, black on chin; female greyish face; easily overlooked

A 877

Montane areas

Brimstone Canary / Dikbekkanarie

Chunkier than most canaries; olive-green above, yellowish below washed olive across the breast; heavy bill, green forecrown, yellow eyestripe, malar stripe and throat

A 878

Yellow Canary / Geelkanarie

Olive streaked above, bright yellow below; yellow eyebrow extending over forecrown, yellow rump, female greyish-brown, streaked below

119

Streaky-headed Seedeater / Streepkopkanarie

Mottled greyish-brown above, buffy-grey below; white crown streaked brown, white eyestripe, white throat

Sparrow

House Sparrow / Huismossie

Snail eggs

Speckled brown above, greyish below; grey crown, nape and rump, horn-coloured bill (black when breeding), smallish black bib

A 802 — Arid areas

Great Sparrow / Grootmossie
Bright chestnut above, white below; grey crown, small white stripe in front of eye, large bold black bib on chest, chestnut rump; shy

A 803

Cape Sparrow / Gewone Mossie
Greyish above, white below; black head with large white C-mark behind the eye, large black bib, rufous shoulder and rump; female with greyish head and thin white eyestripe

A 804

Southern Grey-headed Sparrow / Gryskopmossie
Brownish above, white below; grey head, white wing bar, rufous wing coverts and rump, frequently hops

A 805

Yellow-throated Petronia / Geelvlekmossie
Brownish above, greyish below; strong pale eyestripe, white chin and sometimes yellow spot on breast, white wing stripes; flicks wings and tail after landing; walks

121

Group 8 – Seed eaters
Weaver-like
Pointed bills.

Bishop
Weaver & Quelea
True Weavers
Widow
Whydah

Bishop

Males have distinctive breeding plumage; resemble females during non-breeding season; distinctive courtship flights.

A 824

Southern Red Bishop / Rooivink

Breeding male bright red, face and underparts black; puffed appearance; non-breeding male and female drab

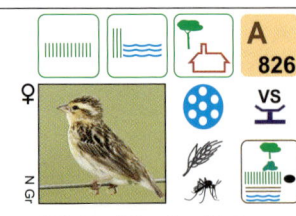

A 826

Yellow-crowned Bishop / Goudgeelvink

Breeding male brilliant yellow crown, back and rump, black below; puffed display; non-breeding male and female mottled brown and dull yellow

A 827

Yellow Bishop / Kaapse Flap

Breeding male black with yellow shoulder, wing coverts and rump, non-breeding males brownish with yellow shoulder and rump, female brownish

Weavers

Differ from true weavers in that they build rough nests from sticks or grass, or weave crude nests.

A 798

Red-billed Buffalo-Weaver / Buffelwewer

Black with flecks of white on wing; red bill, female more brown and mottled below; loves feeding on ground; builds large untidy communal stick nests

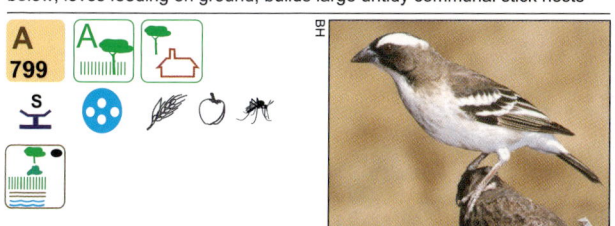

A 799

White-browed Sparrow-Weaver / Koringvoël

Brownish above, white below; dark head with broad white eyebrow, prominent white rump; feeds on ground; noisy; untidy grass nests

Red-billed Quelea / Rooibekkwelea
Black and buff above, white below; male black face mask surrounded by yellow or pink, red bill (female yellow when breeding), female drab; form huge flocks and drink towards evening

True Weavers

Mostly yellow in breeding season with or without facial mask; non-breeding males resemble females; mostly gregarious; colonial breeders; intricate woven nests.

Thick-billed Weaver / Dikbekwewer
Male chocolate brown; thick black bill, white forehead, white marks on primaries, female lighter above, white streaked brown below, yellowish bill and gape; polygynous

A 810

Sometimes single nest
Also nests with short entrances

Spectacled Weaver / Brilwewer

Olive-green above, golden-yellow below; sharp pointed bill, orange shading on head, pale eye, black eyestripe, black bib (male only)

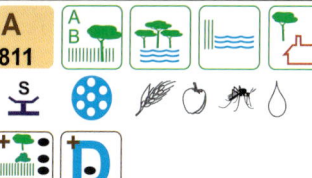

A 811

Village Weaver / Bontrugwewer

Yellow; spotted back, red eye, yellow forehead, black face and throat ending in distinct point, female and non-breeding male throat and breast soft yellow

125

A 813

Cape Weaver / Kaapse Wewer

Olive-green above, bright yellow below; long pointed black bill, rufous wash on the face, yellow eye; flicks wings viciously when alarmed; aggressive

A 814

Southern Masked-Weaver / Swartkeelgeelvink

Olive-green above with plain back, bright yellow below; black forehead and face, red eye, black throat, pink-brown legs; also found in drier areas

126

A 815

Lesser Masked-Weaver / Kleingeelvink

Yellowish-green above, bright yellow below; black forehead and throat, yellow eye, bluish legs

A 816

Golden Weaver / Goudwewer

Greenish-gold above, bright yellow below; large black bill, pale yellow eye, throat and breast sometimes with orange wash, host to Diderick Cuckoo (p. 186)

127

A 818

Southern Brown-throated Weaver / Bruinkeelwewer
Bright yellow tinged olive on back; eyes red-brown, chestnut-brown throat and upper breast, short yellow tail, female olive above, light yellow below; nest without tunnel entrance

A 819

Red-headed Weaver / Rooikopwewer
Scarlet head, breast and mantle, white belly; orange-red bill, brownish wings; female and non-breeding male with yellowish head

Widowbird

Males have distinctive black breeding plumage but look like females in non-breeding season; distinctive display flights; polygynous.

A 828

Fan-tailed Widowbird / Kortstertflap
Black; orange-red shoulders on wings, brown eyes, bluish bill, longish broad tail, female and non-breeding male mottled brown, non-breeding male retains red shoulder patches; fans tail during display flights

A 829

Non-breeding ♂

White-winged Widowbird / Witvlerkflap
Black with yellow shoulder and white band on wing; light blue bill, longish broad tail; displays with fluffed neck feathers and fanned tail; female drab

129

Red-collared Widowbird / Rooikeelflap

Black with red band across throat, black bill, eye and feet, long tail; display flight with rustling wings

Non-breeding male drab; female tawny above with black blotches, buff below, pinkish bill, yellow eyebrow

Long-tailed Widowbird / Langstertflap

Black with large red shoulder patch and white markings on wings; pale blue-grey bill, very long thick and heavy tail, making flight difficult; slow flapping courtship flight; also known as Sakabula.

Female drab brown and streaked; difficult to distinguish from other species

Non-breeding male orange on shoulder

Whydah

Males have very distinctive breeding plumage and long tails; females drab; parasitic and polygynous.

A 860

Common Waxbill

Pin-tailed Whydah / Koningrooibekkie

Breeding male black and white with red bill; long tail; non-breeding male and female drab; aggressive behaviour; dances in the air

A 861

Violet-eared Waxbill

Shaft-tailed Whydah / Pylstertrooibekkie

Male black and tawny coloured with red bill; long tail feathers ending as racquets, non-breeding male and female drab with pinkish bill and square tail

Green-winged Pytilia
(Melba Finch)

Long-tailed Paradise-Whydah / Gewone Paradysvink

Male black with golden nape, rufous breast and yellow belly; broad long tail with two raised rounded feathers below the rump; tail tapers to a point; non-breeding male and female drab; hovers

Group 8 – Seed eaters
Waxbill-like
Very small birds.

Finch
Firefinch
Indigobird
Mannikin

Pytilia (Melba)
Twinspot
Waxbill

Finch

Small birds with short conical bills adapted for seed eating.

A 806

Scaly-feathered Finch / Baardmannetjie

Forehead spotted black and white, pink bill, prominent black malar stripes, wings and tail with white edging around the black feathers; noisy

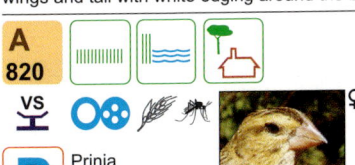

A 820

Prinia and cisticola

Cuckoo Finch / Koekoekvink

Stubby yellow bird resembling finches; heavy bill (black when breeding); wings black with feathers edged yellow; short tail; roosts in reeds; nomadic

133

African Quailfinch / Gewone Kwartelvinkie

Grey above, chestnut below; red bill, large white eyerings, barred breast and flanks; very short tail; active but unobtrusive; ground dwelling

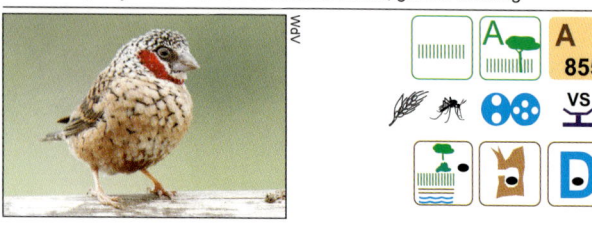

Cut-throat Finch / Bandkeelvink

Light brown above, buff below; barred and mottled black, male white chin with red throat band, females without red throat

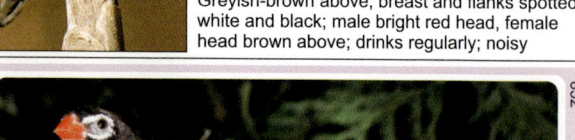

Red-headed Finch / Rooikopvink

Greyish-brown above, breast and flanks spotted white and black; male bright red head, female head brown above; drinks regularly; noisy

Firefinch

Small crimson coloured birds with red rumps; lightly spotted with white on sides of breast; usually small groups feeding on the ground.

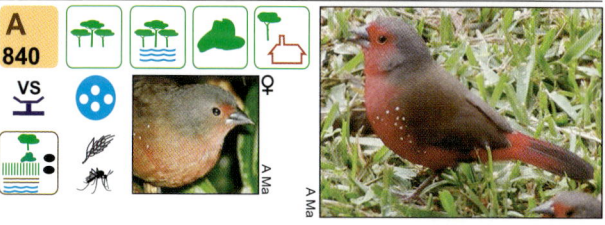

A 840

African Firefinch / Kaapse Vuurvinkie

Dark grey-brown above, red below; slatish black bill, centre of belly and undertail greyish black; female grey face and tawny below

A 841

Jameson's Firefinch / Jamesonse Vuurvinkie

Mostly red with red-brown wings; blue-black bill and legs, female lighter red and barred black under the tail

A 842

Red-billed Firefinch / Rooibekvuurvinkie

Brown above, red below with white spots; red bill, yellow or white eyering, red legs, female buff except for red rump

135

Indigobird

Males very distinct blue-black breeding plumage with brown flight and tail feathers but drab and like females with boldly striped heads in non-breeding plumage; may mimic hosts' song and alarm calls.

A 864

African Firefinch

Dusky Indigobird / Gewone Blouvinkie

Blue-black with white bill and red legs and feet; dominant indigobird along the moist escarpment

A 865

Jameson's Firefinch

Purple Indigobird / Witpootblouvinkie

Blue-black; light pink bill, slightly darker pink legs and feet

A 867

Red-billed Firefinch

Village Indigobird / Staalblouvinkie

Blue-black with red bill, legs and feet; most widespread of indigobirds; distinctive male courtship display

136

Mannikin

Sexes alike; unique bat-like appearance in flight; typically feed on grass stems; may use old weaver, bishop or waxbill nests, often close to a wasp nest; water dependent.

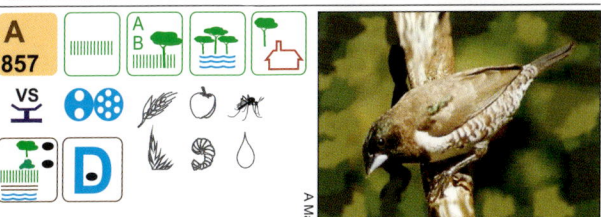

Bronze Mannikin / Gewone Fret

Brown above and white below with barring on flanks and undertail; darker face, forehead washed dull metallic green; wing with green metallic spots

Red-backed Mannikin / Rooirugfret

Black head, mantle and breast, chestnut back and wings, white below; silvery beak, black and white barring and speckling on flanks, wings and rump

Pytilia (Melba)

Orange-winged Pytilia / Oranjevlerkmelba
Golden-olive back, olive and white barring below; red face and ear coverts with grey around the eye, grey upper breast, orange wing tips, female without red on face; rare; nomadic

Green-winged Pytilia / Gewone Melba
Forecrown and throat scarlet, hindcrown and nape grey, wash of green on breast, back and wings golden olive, barred grey and white below, red rump; female similar but with grey head and face; secretive

138

Twinspot

A 835

Green Twinspot / Groenkolpensie

Olive-green above, black below with small white spots; black bill with orange tip, red face, dull orange rump, female yellowish face; secretive

A 838 Sandy soil

Pink-throated Twinspot / Rooskeelkolpensie

Olive-brown above, black below with small pinkish-white spots; brown crown, pinkish face, throat and breast, lower rump dull red; female light grey face; uncommon

139

Waxbill

Small birds; conical bills for eating seeds, bright and colourful plumage; often found in small flocks.

Blue Waxbill / Gewone Blousysie

A 844

Grey-brown above, light blue below with white belly; tail dark blue, female paler blue than male; often nests near a wasp nest for protection

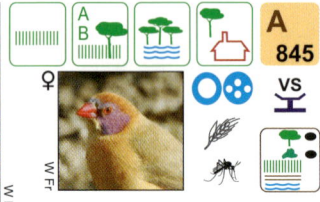

Violet-eared Waxbill / Koningblousysie

A 845

Male rich brown; violet face and bright blue forehead, red bill and red eyering, black throat and centre belly, female paler

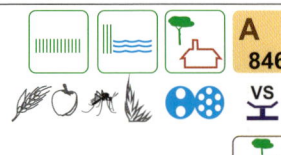

Common Waxbill / Rooibeksysie

A 846

Grey above, pinkish-white with fine barring below; red bill and eyestripe, red in centre of belly, black undertail; flicks tail from side to side

140

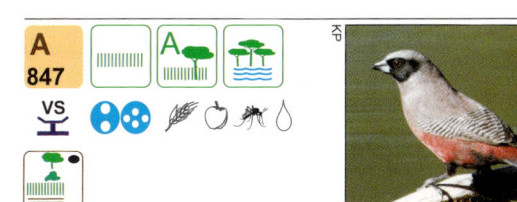

Black-faced Waxbill / Swartwangsysie

Reddish-grey above, chestnut below; chin and ear coverts black, finely barred black and white on the wings, reddish-brown rump; sexes alike

Grey Waxbill / Gryssysie

Also old weaver nests

Grey; black stripe through red eye, blue bill with grey tip, crimson lower back and rump, lower belly slate, black tail

Swee Waxbill / Suidelike Swie

Olive-green back and wings, pale yellow below; grey crown, nape and breast, black face and throat, bill black above and red below, red rump, black tail; female without black face

Orange-breasted Waxbill / Rooiassie

Olive-grey above, orange to yellow below; red bill, eyebrow, rump and undertail, barred on the flanks; restless; constantly flicking tail and wings

141

Group 9 – Mixed feeders
Barbet-like
Strong heavy bills.

Barbet and Tinkerbird
Roller

Barbet and Tinkerbird
Largely living on fruit; very vocal; nest in holes in trees; mainly found in forest and bush habitats.

Black-collared Barbet / Rooikophoutkapper
Olive-grey above, dull yellow-grey below; large black bill, bright red head and throat, black collar and hindcrown; call in duet with much quivering, swaying and bowing; rare form with yellow face

Acacia Pied Barbet / Bonthoutkapper
Dark spotted above, white below; large black bill, black and white striped head, red forehead, short yellow eyebrow, black patch on chest

Yellow-fronted Tinkerbird / Geelblestinker

Black above streaked yellow, pale yellow below; striped face, deep yellow to orange forehead; known for its anvil-tapping calls, "tink-tink-tink"

Yellow-rumped Tinkerbird / Swartblestinker

Head and back black, yellowish below; long white eyebrow and malar stripes, wing feathers yellow edged black, yellow rump and outertail feathers

Mistletoe

Crested Barbet / Kuifkophoutkapper

Speckled white and black above, yellow below; large pale yellow bill, black, red and yellow crested head, broad black breast band, red rump, black tail

Roller

Stoutly built birds with striking plumage, strong bills, hooked at the tip, short legs; will perch on dead trees or on structures out in the open for long periods; habit of turning over in the air like a tumbler pigeon, hence its name.

European Roller / Europese Troupant

Mostly green-blue with brown back and wings; splash of blue on shoulder; square-ended tail; usually quiet

Lilac-breasted Roller / Gewone Troupant

Mostly brown above, blue below; pale green crown and nape, lilac breast, blue rump; long tail with two streamers; harsh squawking

Racket-tailed Roller / Knopsterttroupant

Brown above, turquoise below; green crown and nape, white forehead, dark blue shoulders and wing tips, elongated blue tail with spatulate tips

A 449

Purple Roller / Groottroupant

Olive-brown above, light purple streaked with white below; large head, broad white eyebrow, blue rump, squarish blue tail

S 450

Broad-billed Roller / Geelbektroupant

Brown above, purple below; conspicuous yellow bill, blue on edge of wings, rump and tail; tail short, very vocal in breeding season

Group 9 – Mixed feeders

Parrot

Strong broad curved beaks.

Stocky birds with powerful and mobile hooked beaks; feet with two toes turned backwards, often used as hands; nest in holes in trees; characterful.

A 362

Afro-montane

Kernels

Cape Parrot / Woudpapegaai
Mostly dull green, brighter on rump and belly, dull olive-brown head and neck, both sexes have orange-scarlet wing edges and thighs, female usually has orange-scarlet forehead; endangered

145

Grey-headed Parrot / Savannepapegaai
Dark green above, lighter green below; head and breast grey, female forehead, bend of wing and thighs bright orange-red

Brown-headed Parrot / Bruinkoppapegaai
Smallish beak; dark green back and wings, light green below; brown head and upper breast, indistinct yellow patches on shoulder, bright yellow underwing, yellow rump; noisy

Meyer's Parrot / Bosveldpapegaai
Brown above, green below; sometimes yellow blotches on the crown, brown breast, shoulders yellow, green rump; yellow underwing

146

Group 9 – Mixed feeders
Mostly Prominent Crests
Crests not always displayed.

Bulbul
Brownbul
Greenbul
Nicator

Mousebird
Trogon
Turaco
Go-away Bird

Bulbul & Nicator

Social birds, hawking insects in flight or scraping on ground; very vocal; easily identified by call.

A 568

Dark-capped Bulbul / Swartoogtiptol
Brown above, dull white below; head black, brown-grey breast, yellow vent; very active and noisy; form mobbing parties when in danger

A 569

Terrestrial Brownbul / Boskrapper
Drab; brown above, pale white below; reddish-brown eye, whitish chin; mostly found on forest floor scraping through dead leaves and debris

Yellow-streaked Greenbul / Geelstreepboskruiper
Olive above, whitish below lightly streaked yellow; slender bill, brown eye, white eyering, grey crown and face, olive on flanks, lifts one wing at a time whilst moving; shy

A 570

Sombre Greenbul / Gewone Willie
Forest bird

Sombrely clad; grey-green; black bill, eye white to pale green; forages in dense tree tops or in thick undergrowth; mostly hiding in foliage

A 572

Yellow-bellied Greenbul / Geelborswillie
Olive-green above, yellowish below; strong black bill, brown cap, reddish eye with prominent white eyelid; skulker; sometimes suns itself at forest edge

A 574

Eastern Nicator / Geelvleknikator
Olive-grey above, buffy white below; heavy bill, yellow eyering, pale yellow spots on wing coverts, yellowish underwing and undertail coverts, longish tail tipped pale yellow; skulker

A 575

Mouse-bird

Smallish greyish birds with very long stiff tails; clamber through the trees like mice; will hang from branches, even when sleeping.

A 424

Speckled Mousebird / Gevlekte Muisvoël
Grey-brown above, buff below, very finely barred; upper bill black, lower bill bluish-white, black around the eye; crash lands in trees; loves sand bathing

A 426

Red-faced Mousebird / Rooiwangmuisvoël

Blue-grey above and sandy coloured below; red bill with black tip, eye surrounded by red skin; legs and feet rose-red

Trogon

Trogons are brightly coloured birds of the forest, hawking insects like flycatchers.

Narina Trogon / Bosloerie

Emerald green above and on head and breast, crimson red below; yellow bill, light blue skin around the eye and the gape, white undertail; perches motionless; secretive

150

Turaco & Go-away Bird

Mostly tree-living birds; run and jump along branches.

A 370

Knysna Turaco / Knysnaloerie

Olive-green; green head with prominent white-tipped crest, red bill and eyering, white stripes above and below eye, blue wash on wings and long tail, crimson flight feathers; restless; runs along branches

A 371

Purple-crested Turaco / Bloukuifloerie
Blue-green above; dark blue-purple crest, wings and tail, metallic green on face, red eyering, pinkish wash on mantle and breast, crimson flight feathers; shy; noisy; runs and jumps along branches

A 373

Grey Go-away-bird / Kwêvoël
Uniformly coloured grey; short stubby bill; long hairy crest often raised; long tail; very vocal

Group 10 – Insect eaters
Batis-like

Small birds, dull to colourful; many have distinguishing calls; sexes mostly similar.

Apalis
Batis & Wattle-eye
Camaroptera
Crombec
Eremomela & Woodland-Warbler

Penduline Tit
Prinia
Titbabbler
White-eye
Wren-Warbler

Apalis
Mainly tree-living; very active; sing in duet.

A 645

Bar-throated Apalis / Bandkeelkleinjantjie
Green-grey above, white to yellowish below; pale eye with small black area below eye, black band across breast, lower belly yellow, white outertail feathers; very variable

A 648

Yellow-breasted Apalis / Geelborskleinjantjie
Greenish above, white below; grey face, red eye, yellow breast, male with black bar on breast; cocks and flicks tail and drops wings; highly vocal

152

A 649

Rudd's Apalis / Ruddse Kleinjantjie
Olive-green above, white below; grey head, dark brown eye, creamy throat, black breast band, lemon-yellow on sides of chest, olive-green tail

Batis & Wattle-eye

Small flycatchers; inhabit forests, woodland and bush; each species has a distinctive call; sexes differ.

A 700

Cape Batis / Kaapse Bosbontrokkie
Grey above, white below; black face, male with broad black breast band, russet wings and flanks; red eye when breeding; female chestnut breast band

A 701

Chinspot Batis / Witliesbosbontrokkie
Grey above, white below; yellow eye, black face with white eyebrow, white wing bar, male black breast band, female chestnut breast band

153

Black-throated Wattle-eye / Beloogbosbontrokkie
Black above, white below; bright red wattles above the eye, male with a narrow black breast band, female with black throat and upper chest and white chin; secretive

Camaroptera

Dull-coloured with slender bills and long legs; prefer dense undergrowth; formerly known as bleating warblers.

Green-backed Camaroptera / Groenrugkwêkwêvoël
Olive-green crown, mantle and back, pale grey below; grey forehead, orange-brown eyes, olive-green wings, short tail held cocked over back; bleating alarm call

Grey-backed Camaroptera / Grysrugkwêkwêvoël
Lead-grey above, pale grey below; orange-brown eye, olive-green wings, short tail held cocked over back; vocal

154

Crombec

Small restless birds of drier areas; sexes alike.

A 651

Long-billed Crombec / Bosveldstompstert
Grey-brown above, tawny-rufous below; long slightly decurved bill, dark eye, tawny eyebrow, dark stripe through the eye; very short tail (seems tailless); has a frequent high-pitched trilling call

Eremomela (Bush-Warbler)

Unobtrusive small warblers; usually heard before they are seen; very active; sexes alike.

A 644

Yellow-throated Woodland-Warbler / Geelkeelsanger
Olive-grey above, greyish belly; rufous crown and eyestripe, yellow eyebrow, face, breast and vent; afro-montane forest habitat; upper canopy feeder

155

Yellow-bellied Eremomela / Geelpensbossanger

Grey-brown above, grey breast and yellowish belly; white eyebrow, dark line through the eye

Green-capped Eremomela / Donkerwangbossanger

Olive-grey above, pale yellow below; red and yellow eye; usually in hilly areas

Burnt-necked Eremomela / Bruinkeelbossanger
Grey-brown above, very light yellow below; bill light coloured below, light eye with a brown eyering, male has a cinnamon bar around the throat during breeding season

Penduline-Tit

Sexes alike; forage in small flocks; build tough waterproof nests tightly felted with woolly plant or animal material with false entrance.

A 557

Cape Penduline-Tit / Kaapse Kapokvoël

Light brownish-grey above, buffy-yellow below; pointed black bill, black forehead speckled white, black eyestripe

A 558

Grey Penduline-Tit / Gryskapokvoël

Pale-grey above, buffy-cinnamon below; shortish bill, lighter throat and breast, flanks brighter, white underwing; calls frequently; more eastern distribution

Prinia

685 Non-breeding

Small brownish birds with long tails mostly cocked; very active and vocal; sexes mostly alike.

A 683

Tawny-flanked Prinia / Bruinsylangstertjie

Greyish-brown above, buffy white to tawny below; buffy eyebrow, wing feathers edged rufous, tail with pale tip

A 685

Black-chested Prinia / Swartbandlangstertjie

Greyish-brown above, lemon-yellow below; male with white eyebrow and throat, broad black chest band during the breeding season

A 949

Drakensberg Prinia / Drakensberglangstertjie

Brownish above, whitish below with a yellow wash and brown streaking on the chest; white eyebrow; long tail often cocked up; bracken stands

158

Tit-Babbler

Noisy; often detected by their call; very active; moving within the canopy; often spread their tails before flying.

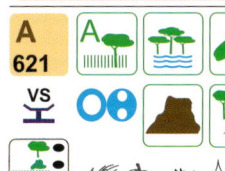

Chestnut-vented Tit-Babbler / Bosveldtjeriktik

Dull blue-grey bird; cream eye, bold streaking on throat, undertail bright chestnut; active; inquisitive and vocal; mimics other birds

White-eye

Tree living, rapidly moving through the foliage in groups; constant twittering.

Cape White-eye / Kaapse Glasogie

Grey-green above, olive-green below; prominent eyering formed by white feathers; yellow throat and undertail

159

African Yellow White-eye / Geelglasogie
Yellow-green above, sulphur yellow below; white eyering; sociable; active leaf gleaner

Wren-Warbler

Small; barred; mostly found in low bush areas, hiding in undergrowth when disturbed; prefer semi-arid areas.

Barred Wren-Warbler / Gebande Sanger
Rich brown above, warm buffy-white below fully barred; brown eye; longish tail usually held fanned over back; brown breast when breeding; ventriloquist

Stierling's Wren-Warbler / Stierlingse Sanger
Rufous-brown above, white below with distinct brown barring from face to undertail; orange-red eye, bold white bars on wing; feeds mostly near or on ground

Group 10 – Insect eaters
Thrush-like
Small bills; ground and rock birds.

Chat
Robin
Thrush
Wheatear

Chat
and allied

A 589

Familiar Chat / Gewone Spekvreter

Drab brownish, off-white on belly; light edge around the eye, chestnut on rump and tail; flicks wings and raises tail, especially when landing; found in rough rocky areas; bold around human settlements

A 593

Mocking Cliff-Chat / Dassievoël

Male with glossy black head, breast and tail, chestnut rump and belly; white mark on the bend of the wing, female slaty-black, chestnut below; excellent singer; shy

161

Miombo & Mopani woodland

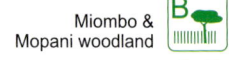

A 594

Arnot's Chat / Bontpiek
Black with white shoulder patch; male with white crown, female with white throat speckled black

A 595

Ant-eating Chat / Swartpiek
Dumpy and upright; male black-brown, white shoulder patch and primaries; female lighter brown; will perch on ant-heap or low structure; nests in dongas or antbear holes

A 596

African Stonechat / Gewone Bontrokkie
Male black above, white below with chestnut breast; black face, white collar, female lighter, brown streaked back and crown; open areas

595 ♀

596 ♀

162

Robin-Chat & Scrub-Robin

Mostly with white eyebrows and rufous rumps; active birds mainly feeding on the ground; often jerk tails up and spread it in typical robin fashion.

A 598

Chorister Robin-Chat / Lawaaimakerjanfrederik
Dark grey above, deep orange below; head, face and middle of tail dark grey, rump and edges of tail orange

A 599

White-browed Robin-Chat / Heuglinse Janfrederik
Greyish-brown above, rich orange below; black crown with prominent white eyebrow; crepuscular; excellent singer; good mimic; shy

A 600

Red-capped Robin-Chat / Nataljanfrederik
Dark blue-grey back and wings, dull orange below; rufous crown, orange face and tail, tail black in centre; shy; feeding on ground, especially at dusk; excellent mimic

163

Montane scrub

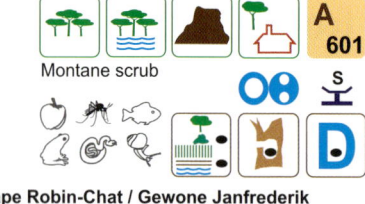

A 601

Cape Robin-Chat / Gewone Janfrederik
Brown-grey above, white-grey belly; black face with white eyestripe, orange-rufous breast, brown and orange tail; very active and vocal; but secretive

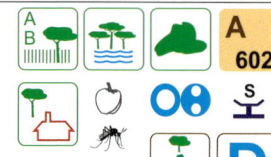

A 602

White-throated Robin-Chat / Witkeeljanfrederik
Blackish-grey above, white below; white eyebrow, chin and throat, white bar on the wing; rufous flanks and rump

Forest floor

A 606

White-starred Robin / Witkoljanfrederik
Dark grey-blue head, throat and wings, olive-brown mantle, orange-yellow below; small white spot above each eye and on throat mainly visible during display, yellow tail with black centre

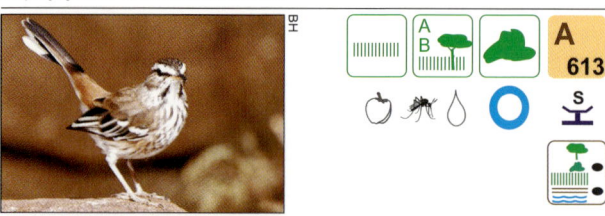

A 613

White-browed Scrub-Robin / Gestreepte Wipstert
Brownish above, white below; bill black above and yellow below, white eyebrow, dark streaks on breast, white bar on the wing, prominent rufous rump, dark tail with a white tip

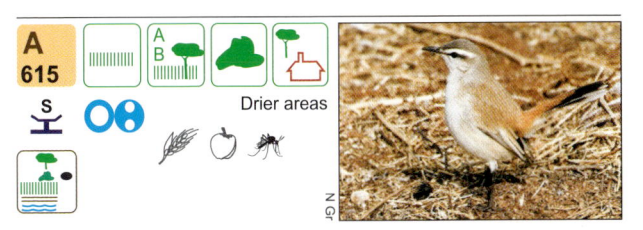

Kalahari Scrub-Robin / Kalahariwipstert
Sandy coloured above, pale below; white eyebrow, distinctive rufous tail with black subterminal band and white tips; longish legs; very upright; mimics

Brown Scrub-Robin / Bruinwipstert

Brown-grey above, white below with grey flanks; white eye and malar stripes, black and white patches on shoulder of wing, white-tipped tail; shy; forages in dark forest patches

Bearded Scrub-Robin / Baardwipstert
Brown above, white below with light rufous breast, flanks and rump; bold white eyebrow bordered black above and below, white malar stripe and throat, white and black marks on wing edge

165

Thrush

Good singers; usually first birds to call at dawn and last to call at night; frequently scratching amongst fallen leaves; aggressive in their territories; sexes alike.

Kurrichane Thrush / Rooibeklyster
Grey above, orange and creamy below; orange bill and eyering, white chin, black malar stripe, legs and feet yellow-orange; bold and confiding in gardens

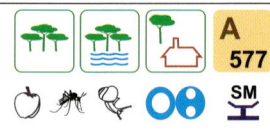

A 576

Olive Thrush / Olyflyster
Similar to 577.1 but with a dark patch around the nostril region and black streaks on the white throat; mostly forest dwelling; some interbreeding with 577.1 occurs

A 577

Karoo Thrush / Geelbeklyster
Dark olive-grey to brown above, dull orange below with grey breast and flanks; bill and nostril area mostly yellow, black streaking on throat; displays with tail spread while wings are dragging on the ground

A 577.1

A 579 Montane forests

Orange Ground-Thrush / Oranjelyster
Dark brown above, orange lores, throat and breast, white belly; white eyering, black bill, two distinct white wing bars; elusive; usually near streams

A 580

Groundscraper Thrush / Gevlekte Lyster
Grey above, spotted white below; yellow bill, black facial markings; flicks one wing at a time; stooped running, stopping in upright position

Palm-Thrush

A 603 Palm thickets

Palm thickets

Collared Palm-Thrush / Palmmôrelyster
Light brown above, greyish below; whitish eye, cream coloured throat with black border, wings, rump and tail rufous; hops on ground with tail cocked; localised

167

Rock-Thrush

Found in rocky mountainous habitat; good singers; take long hops between rocks; flick wings and spread tails.

Rocky gorges **A 581**

Cape Rock-Thrush / Kaapse Kliplyster
Male blue-grey head, rest rich rufous; female head speckled buffy-brown; rest orange-rufous

A 583

Short-toed Rock-Thrush / Korttoonkliplyster
Male blue-grey above, orange-rufous below; whitish crown, slate blue head and throat, orange tail with black centre; female pale brown above, orange below with striped throat

Wheatear

Perch upright; nest in old rodent or mongoose burrows or holes in rock faces, walls or buildings.

Mountain Wheatear / Bergwagter
586

Much variation; males mostly black, sometimes with a white belly; males with grey or white crowns and napes, white shoulder patch and rump, white outertail feathers, females blackish-brown; prefers rocky areas; nomadic

Capped Wheatear / Hoëveldskaapwagter
587

Russet-brown above, white below; black head with white eyebrow and chin, broad black breast band, cinnamon rump; sexes alike

Buff-streaked Chat / Bergklipwagter
588

Mostly black above, orange-buff below; black head, broad buff eyestripe, V-shaped white band on back; female brownish; nomadic

169

Group 10 – Insect eaters
Hoopoe-like

Small-medium birds; black slender curved bills.

Bee-eater
Hoopoe
Wood-hoopoe

Bee-eater

Colourful aerial feeders; long dark streak through eye; group-forming, sleeping shoulder to shoulder; nest in tunnels in sand banks; call whilst flying; sunbathe; interesting ceremonies and displays.

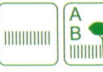

Colony in Northwest Province

European Bee-eater / Europese Byvreter

Warm brown above, light blue below; yellow throat with black collar, yellow rump, longish tail; very vocal in the air

Blue-cheeked Bee-eater / Blouwangbyvreter

Mainly dirty green colour; bluish forehead, red-brown eye, yellow chin, brown throat; centre tail elongated

441

Southern Carmine Bee-eater / Rooiborsbyvreter

Mostly rose-red; green-blue head, soft blue rump and lower belly, tail with elongated central tail feathers; may ride on backs of animals and birds

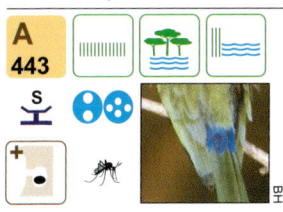

443

White-fronted Bee-eater / Rooikeelbyvreter

Green above, bronze below; forehead and chin white, red throat, bright blue rump, square blue-green tail

444

Sometimes in roofs of antbear holes

Little Bee-eater / Kleinbyvreter

Olive-green above, cinnamon-yellow below; yellow throat, black band across throat, tail squarish or slightly forked with broad terminal band

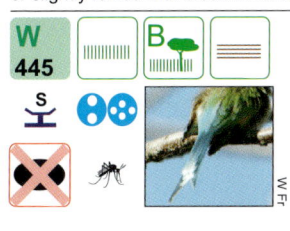

445

Swallow-tailed Bee-eater / Swaelstertbyvreter

Mostly green; red eye, yellow throat enclosed by blue band, blue rump, deeply forked tail

171

Hoopoe and Wood-Hoopoe

Striking birds; probe for insects with long curved bills. Wood-Hoopoes have long tails.

A 451

African Hoopoe / Hoephoep
Overall cinnamon coloured; long crest frequently fanned out, black and white barred wings, white rump; walks with quick short steps and nodding head; rolling flight action

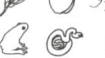

A 452

Green Wood-Hoopoe / Rooibekkakelaar
Bright iridescent blue-green plumage; red bill, two white patches on the wing, long tail with white spots, red legs and feet; restless

A 454

Common Scimitarbill / Swartbekkakelaar
Overall black with purple sheen; heavily curved black bill, white patch on the wing, long tail, sometimes with white spots on undertail, black legs; partial to drier areas

Group 10 – Insect eaters
Hornbill & Ground-Hornbill
Curved and heavy bills.

Hornbill
Ground-Hornbill

Hornbill
Large somewhat clumsy birds with heavy bills, sometimes with extra growth or casque in males; short legs, long tails; sexes much alike; females imprisoned in hole in tree during breeding.

A 455

Trumpeter Hornbill / Gewone Boskraai
Black above, white below; black face and upper breast, pinkish skin around the eye, huge blackish casqued bill, white wing edge and rump, long black tail tipped white; very vocal

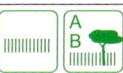

A 457

African Grey Hornbill / Grysneushoringvoël
Dull grey above, whitish below; black bill, ridges on lower mandible, white eyebrow, female upper bill light yellow with red tip; whistling call

173

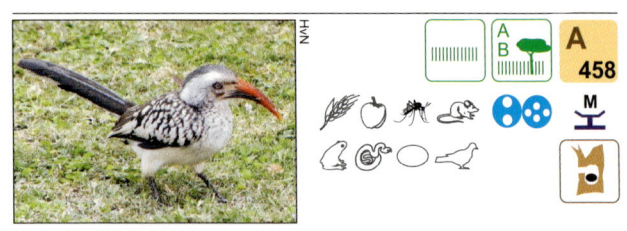

Red-billed Hornbill / Rooibekneushoringvoël
Grey above, white below; red bill, black cap, white eyebrow, yellow or brown eyes, skin around eyes pink, mottled wings, black tail with white outertail feathers

Southern Yellow-billed Hornbill / Geelbekneushoringvoël
Greyish with black and white markings above, white below; big yellow bill, yellow eyes surrounded by dark pink skin; white outertail feathers

Crowned Hornbill / Gekroonde Neushoringvoël
Dark brown above, dark grey breast and throat, white below; feathers tipped white on head and neck, orange-red bill with narrow yellow base, yellow eye, white outertail feathers

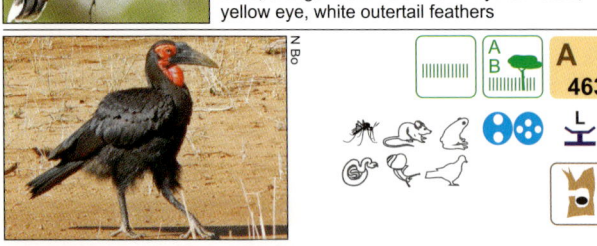

Southern Ground-Hornbill / Bromvoël
Black turkey-like bird; large black bill, yellow eyes, bright red skin around the eyes and neck, female smaller with blue patch on throat; deep resonant booming call

174

Group 10 – Insect eaters
Nightjar
Short bill, wide gape, large eyes.

All have typical bark and dead leaf cryptic plumage. Nocturnal birds; spend the day hiding on the ground, amongst bushes or on rocks. All have long wings and tails and a wide gape for catching insects on the wing. Very vocal at night. Difficult to distinguish between species.

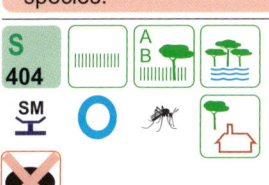

S 404

European Nightjar / Europese Naguil
Male shows white on the wing and tail, female no white markings on wing or tail; rests lengthwise along a horizontal branch; silent in South Africa

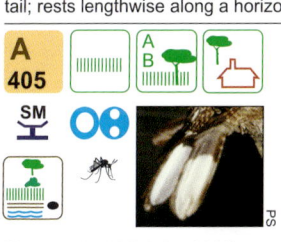

A 405

Fiery-necked Nightjar / Afrikaanse Naguil
Rufous collar that extends around the neck; broad black streak on the centre of the crown, female off-white tips to outertail feathers; call: "Good Lord deliver us"

S 406

Rufous-cheeked Nightjar / Rooiwangnaguil
Rufous cheek during breeding season, some black on the crown, little white on wing and tail tips; call – series of coughs and continuous churring sounds without variation

175

Freckled Nightjar / Donkernaguil
Freckled brown above that blends in with rocky terrain, white innertail feathers; sometimes roosting on buildings in towns and cities; call – yaps like a small dog

Square-tailed Nightjar / Laeveldnaguil
Rufous around the neck; spotted white on ends of secondaries wing feathers, white on full length of outertail feathers; call – trill, varying in pitch

Pennant-winged Nightjar / Wimpelvlerknaguil
Breeding male with long trailing pennants and broad white band across wing, no white on tail, female more rufous wings without pennants and white wingbar, also no white on tail; batlike twittering call

Group 10 – Insect eaters
Oriole-like
Medium birds, straight bills.

Babbler
Cuckooshrike
Drongo
Oriole
Woodpecker
Wryneck

Babbler
Stoutly built; strong bills; long and strong legs; very vocal; forage in small groups.

A 560

Arrow-marked Babbler / Pylvlekkatlagter
Dark brown above, ashy brown below with pointed white arrows; eyes with orange and yellow rings; long tail with rounded end; very noisy

A 563

Southern Pied Babbler / Witkatlagter
Mainly white with black wings and tail; black bill, orange eyes; mostly feeding on the ground; noisy; occurs in semi-arid savanna areas

Cuckooshrike

Very shy and unobtrusive birds of the forest and thick bush.

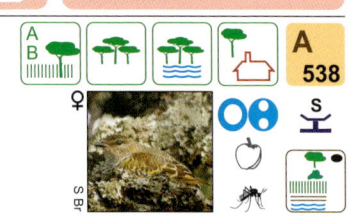

A 538

Black Cuckooshrike / Swartkatakoeroe

Male black, sometimes with bright yellow patch on wing; black bill, yellow-orange gape, female yellowish-olive above, white below barred black

A 539

White-breasted Cuckooshrike / Witborskatakoeroe

Light grey above, white below; black lore and eye, male grey throat, female white throat; tree canopy dweller; hawks insects

A 540

Grey Cuckooshrike / Bloukatakoeroe

Grey all over; white ring around large black eye, male with black lore; upper tree canopy dweller; hawks insects; mostly quiet

Drongo

Often perch on vantage points from where they will dash out after prey, also on ground, returning to same perch; fearless; will loudly attack and dive-bomb larger birds; sexes alike.

A 541

Fork-tailed Drongo / Mikstertbyvanger

Purplish-black; black bill, red eye, wing tips translucent, longish tail deeply notched, very vocal; may hawk from animal backs; mimics

A 542

Square-tailed Drongo / Kleinbyvanger
Smaller than 541; black; red eye, square or slightly notched tail, dark flight feathers; aggressive; highly vocal; evergreen forest resident

179

Oriole

Plumage mostly yellow, usually with black and white markings; red bills and eyes; secretive, spending much time in tree canopies.

Eurasian Golden Oriole / Europese Wielewaal
Male mostly yellow; wings mostly black with a yellow spot, female yellowish-green above, streaked yellowish-white below; shy; mostly silent in South Africa

African Golden Oriole / Afrikaanse Wielewaal
Male mostly yellow; black eyestripe extending behind the eye, black wing tips, female yellowish-green above, dull yellow below; shy

Black-headed Oriole / Swartkopwielewaal
Bright yellow with black head and breast; some black on wings and tail, small white spot on wings; sexes alike; liquid flute-like call

Woodpecker

Streaked olive-brown above and white below; sometimes hanging upside down under branches; will tap branches for food and communication. Work their way upwards in trees.

A 481

Bennett's Woodpecker / Bennettse Speg

Dark red eye, male red cap and malar streaks, spotted below, female speckled forehead, red nape, brown throat and facial patches; feeds on ground on ants and termites

A 483

Golden-tailed Woodpecker / Goudstertspeg

Male red eye, hindcrown and malar stripes, streaky breast, female black crown spotted white, red nape; loud and distinct nasal call

A 486

Cardinal Woodpecker / Kardinaalspeg

Small bill; reddish eye, male red crown, female black crown and nape, both sexes have brown foreheads, black malar stripes and streaked breasts

181

Bearded Woodpecker / Baardspeg

Long sharp bill, speckled forehead, black ear patches and malar stripes, diagonal barring below, male red crown, female black crown; very loud call and branch tapping

Olive Woodpecker / Gryskopspeg

Yellowish olive-green above with red rump, dull green below; no speckling; male grey head with red crown, female grey head

Wryneck

Red-throated Wryneck / Draaihals

Brown barred and mottled plumage with dark chestnut throat and upper breast, white belly streaked black; feeds mostly on the ground, hopping around; frequently found in exotic trees

182

Group 10 – Insect eaters
Shrike-like
Small to medium birds, curved and hooked bills.

Cuckoo
Shrike

Cuckoo
(Large)
Stoutly built; longish bills; pointed wings; longish tails; parasitic; most have loud calls.

S 374

Common Cuckoo / Europese Koekoek

Grey above with white barred belly; bill yellow base with black tip, eye orange to pale brown, yellow eyering; shy; silent in South Africa

S 375

P Fork-tailed Drongo

African Cuckoo / Afrikaanse Koekoek

Dark grey above, white barred below; bill mainly yellow-orange with black tip, yellow eyering, undertail barred; diagnostic two-syllable call

Red-chested Cuckoo / Piet-my-vrou

Dark grey above, white barred below; dark eye with yellowish eyering, chestnut upper breast; shy, sits well hidden; well-known "Piet-my-vrou" call

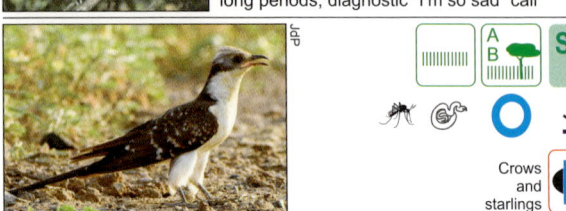

Robin-Chat, wagtail, etc.

Black Cuckoo / Swartkoekoek

Black with a green gloss; shy; sits hunched for long periods; diagnostic "I'm so sad" call

Fork-tailed Drongo, Crimson-breasted Shrike, boubou, etc.

Great Spotted Cuckoo / Gevlekte Koekoek

Dark spotted above, whitish below; red-orange eyering, grey face and crest, buff throat and upper breast, juvenile dark cap and chestnut primaries; noisy

Crows and starlings

Levaillant's Cuckoo / Gestreepte Nuwejaarsvoël

Dark above, white below; black crest, black striping in front, white patch on the primaries, black tail tipped white; noisy; also black morph

Babblers

184

S 382

Bulbul, Common Fiscal, Fork-tailed Drongo, etc.

Jacobin Cuckoo / Bontnuwejaarsvoël

Black above, white below; head crested; short white wing bar, black tail tipped white; also a dark morph

S 383

Retz's Helmet-Shrike

Thick-billed Cuckoo / Dikbekkoekoek

Dark grey above, white below; bill black above, yellow below, undertail barred, female lighter grey above with mottled head

Cuckoo (Small)

Sexes differ.

S 384

White-starred Robin, camaroptera

African Emerald Cuckoo / Mooimeisie

Bright metallic green above and on breast, bright yellow below; white undertail barred green, female brownish, barred above and below

185

Klaas's Cuckoo / Meitjie
Glossy green above, white below; greenish bill, white patch behind the eye, white outertail feathers, female brownish bars above and below; distinctive "Meitjie-Meitjie" call

Forest edge

Weavers, sparrows, finches

Diderick Cuckoo / Diederikkie

Glossy green with copper sheen above, white below; male red eye and eye-ring, broad white eyestripe, white stripe on mid-crown, white marks on wings, barring on flanks, female more bronze; distinctive "dee-dee-dee-diderick" call

Shrike

Strongly built with strong hooked bills; mostly reluctant fliers; referred to as "Butcher-birds" mainly because of their carnivorous habit and impaling of food on thorns, fences etc.

Lesser Grey Shrike / Gryslaksman
731

Adult male pearl-grey above, white below; broad black eyestripe, pink flush on the breast, black primaries; mainly frequents semi-arid areas

Common Fiscal / Fiskaallaksman
732

Black above, white below; white patches on wing form V-mark on the back; longish tail; upright stance; female small rufous patch on flank

Red-backed Shrike / Rooiruglaksman
733

Chestnut back, white below; blue-grey crown and rump, broad black eyestripe, female brown ear patch; frequent tail movement

187

Magpie Shrike / Langstertlaksman

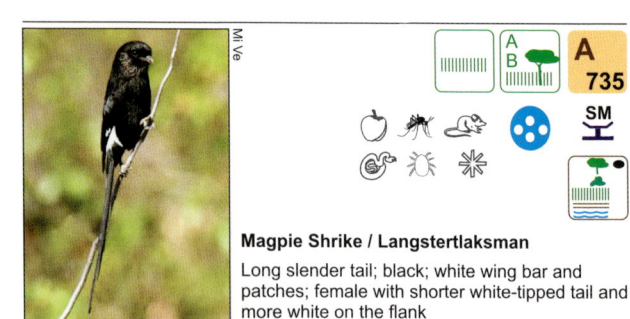

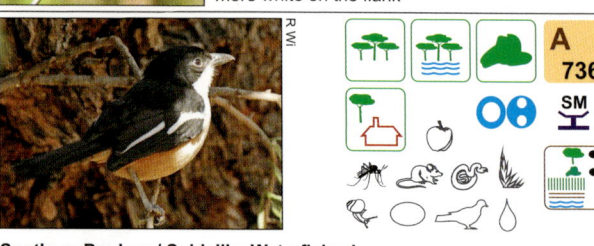

Long slender tail; black; white wing bar and patches; female with shorter white-tipped tail and more white on the flank

Southern Boubou / Suidelike Waterfiskaal

Black above, white to cinnamon below; white patches on wing forming V on the back; shortish rounded tail; secretive; very vocal, call in duet

Tropical Boubou / Tropiese Waterfiskaal

Black above, white below tinged pink; slender bill; call in duet; easily confused with 736

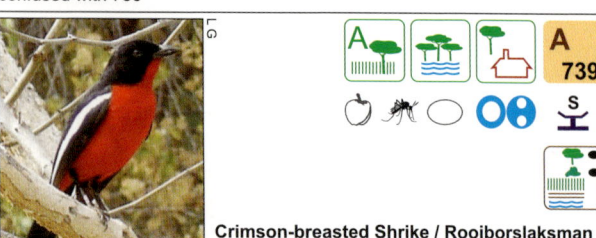

Crimson-breasted Shrike / Rooiborslaksman

Jet black above with white wing stripes forming V on the back, crimson below; call in duet; forages in shrubbery; hops; rare yellow form

188

A 740

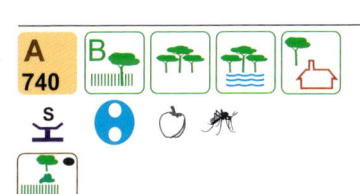

Black-backed Puffback / Sneeubal
Black above, white below; black cap, red eye, grey wing, long white hairy feathers on lower back displayed as a powder-puff, female lighter; vocal; forages high in trees

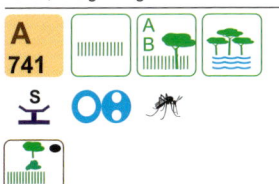

A 741

Brubru / Bontroklaksman

Black and white above, white below; black cap, white eyebrow, bright chestnut markings on the flanks; vocal

A 743

Brown-crowned Tchagra / Rooivlerktjagra

Crown and back brown, buff below; wide white eyebrow bordered with black stripes, rufous wings, black tail tipped white; vocal; spends much time on the ground; shy

A 744

Black-crowned Tchagra / Swartkroontjagra

Brown above, pale grey below; black crown and forehead, white eyebrow, black eyestripe, rufous wings, black tail tipped white; vocal; prefers wooded areas; shy

189

Bokmakierie
Greenish-yellow above, yellow below with prominent black breast band that stetches through the eye to the bill; grey crown, broad yellow eyebrow, black eyestripe, tail black with broad yellow tip; sing in duet

Grey-headed Bush-Shrike / Spookvoël

Largest shrike; yellow-green above, bright yellow below with orange wash on the breast; very strong black bill, grey head and mantle, yellow eye

Bats

White-crested Helmet-Shrike / Withelmlaksman

Black above with white wing stripes, white below; grey crown, yellow eye with yellow serrated eye-wattles, white collar, forages in small groups

Retz's Helmet-Shrike / Swarthelmlaksman

Blackish-brown above, black below; bill, eyering and legs red, white undertail, white-tipped tail; aggressive

A 756 — Baobab trees

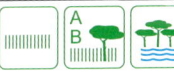

Southern White-crowned Shrike / Kremetartlaksman
Greyish-brown above, white below; white crown, black eyestripe, cheeks, hind neck, wing and tail; hunts from perch

Group 10 – Insect eaters

Starling-like

Small birds, slender bills.

Bush-Shrike
Broadbill
Hyliota

Flycatcher
Starling
Tit

Bush-Shrike

Mostly green and yellow tree-living birds; gleaning leaves and twigs for food; shy; very good singers.

A 747

Gorgeous Bush-Shrike / Konkoit
Olive-green above, yellow below; yellow eyebrow, bright red throat bordered by black collar that extends to the lores, orange vent; skulker in dense thickets

Orange-breasted Bush-Shrike / Oranjeborsboslaksman

Grey and green above, yellow below with an orange breast; yellow forehead and eyebrow, black lores; skulking and moving among vegetation

Black-fronted Bush-Shrike / Swartoogboslaksman

Yellow-green above, deep orange below; prominent black eyestripe, dark blue-grey crown and nape, tail green; upper canopy dweller

Olive Bush-Shrike / Olyfboslaksman

Olive-green above, buffy-pink below; head, neck and mantle blue-grey, black face mask, variable white eyebrow and malar stripe, blackish tail, female duller and faintly barred

192

Flycatcher
& related species

Large varied family of insect eaters mostly hawking from perches; all have big eyes; some have stiff bristles around the bills; sexes alike.

A 490

African Broadbill / Breëbek
Greyish-brown above, creamy-white below, heavily streaked on breast and flanks; brown streaked crown, broad flat bill dark above, pale below; unusual display flight

A 624

Southern Hyliota / Mashonahyliota
Matt blue-black above, creamy yellow below; short white wing bar, white outertail feathers, female brownish-grey above; quiet; uncommon

S 689

Spotted Flycatcher / Europese Vlieëvanger
Dull brownish-grey above, whitish below lightly striped; streaks on head; flicks wings on return to perch; sits quietly with head drawn into shoulders

193

A 690

African Dusky Flycatcher / Donkervlieëvanger

Smoky grey above, cream to white below indistinctly streaked on breast and flanks; buffy white eyering and short eyebrow; shortish wings; sometimes flicks wings on perching

A 691

Ashy Flycatcher / Blougrysvlieëvanger

Pale blue-grey above, lighter grey below shading to white on belly and vent; dark bill, white eyering, black lore, grey tail; flicks wings on returning to perch

A 693

Grey Tit-Flycatcher / Waaierstertvlieëvanger

Grey plumage, paler below; tail black with white outertail feathers; lowers and raises tail whilst fanning it; gleans food from leaves and twigs like a warbler

A 694

Old bird's nests, aloe leaves, banana bunches

Southern Black Flycatcher / Swartvlieëvanger

Glossy blue-black; slender bill and black eye, translucent flight feathers on wing, slightly notched tail, female brownish mottled throat and breast

A 695

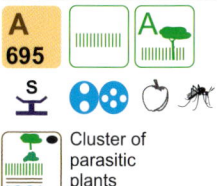

Cluster of parasitic plants

Marico Flycatcher / Maricovlieëvanger
Brown above, silky white below; white eyering, buff wing panel; perches low; also takes prey from the ground

A 696

Pale Flycatcher / Muiskleurvlieëvanger
Grey-brown above, paler buffy-grey below; white chin; perches low; also takes prey from the ground; occasionally hawks; flicks wings and tail

W 698

Breeds elsewhere in South Africa

Fiscal Flycatcher / Fiskaalvlieëvanger
Black above, white below; slender bill; white wing bars not reaching shoulders, shortish tail with white streaks, female brownish above; mimics other birds

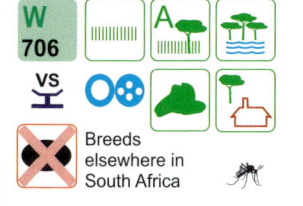

W 706

Breeds elsewhere in South Africa

Fairy Flycatcher / Feevlieëvanger
Blue-grey; black face mask, white eyebrow, breast soft grey, black wings with white wing bar, pinkish belly, white outertail feathers; fans and bobs tail

Blue-mantled Crested-Flycatcher / Bloukuifvlieëvanger
Head with crest; glossy blue-black above, white below with black breast; white patch on wing, longish round tail; very active; fans tail; twists and turns on perch

African Paradise-Flycatcher / Paradysvlieëvanger

Chestnut above, steel-blue crested head, mantle, throat and breast, bright blue gape and eyering, long chestnut tail; female mostly short tail; very vocal and active

196

Starling

Medium-sized birds mostly with a brilliant metallic sheen on their plumage; sturdy bills; some species are gregarious, especially when roosting; each species has distinctive calls and behaviour.

Common Myna / Indiese Spreeu
Dark brown above, brown below; yellow bill, facial skin, legs and feet, white flight feathers and undertail; noisy; vocal at roost; aggressive; mimics; invader

Wattled Starling / Lelspreeu
Grey above and whitish below; primaries black, white rump; breeding male's head decorated with yellow and black skin and wattles; vocal; nomadic

Violet-backed Starling / Witborsspreeu
Glossy amethyst head, back and upper breast, white below; yellow eye, female brownish above, white spotted brown below, always yellow gape

197

Burchell's Starling / Grootglansspreeu

Brilliant metallic blue-green; blackish face and ear coverts, long rounded purplish tail; walks like a crow; sings well

Meves's Starling / Langstertglansspreeu

Slender; glossy blue-bronze above, purple wash over blue belly; dark brown eyes, black ear coverts, long graduated and pointed tail with black barring

Cape Glossy Starling / Kleinglansspreeu

Iridescent blue-green with purple and blue reflections; orange-yellow eye, lacks darker ear coverts of other species; bold and noisy

Greater Blue-eared Starling / Grootblouoorglansspreeu

Bright metallic blue-green sheen above, royal blue below; eye bright orange, broad blue-black ear patch, two rows of black spots on wing

Caves, mine shafts, base of palm fronds

Red-winged Starling / Rooivlerkspreeu
Blue-black plumage with metallic sheen; rich rufous primaries visible in flight; longish tail; female dark grey head

Tit

Small birds with strong bills and white outertail feathers; feeds on insects and fruit in canopies of trees, even hanging upside down; very active; harsh ringing call.

Ashy Tit / Akasiagrysmees
Light bluish-grey back and wings, white below; black head with black stretching to belly, white stripe below eye; inquisitive feeder; calls frequently

Southern Black Tit / Gewone Swartmees
Black; white wing stripes and outertail feathers, female lead-grey below; rambles around in small noisy parties

199

Group 10 – Insect eaters

Swallow-like

Mostly aerial birds.

Martin
Swallow
Saw-wing

Swift
Spinetail
Pratincole

Martin
(Mostly brown martins)

Compact birds with broad wings; slow leisurely flight.

A 529

Rock Martin / Kransswael

All brown; darker above, lighter below; only martin with white windows in the square fanned tail; call a melodious twitter

S 530

Common House-Martin / Huisswael

Looks like a swallow; blue back and head, white below; white rump, black tail slightly forked, white leggings extending to pink feet; rather fluttering flight; congregates near cliffs or high structures

200

S 532

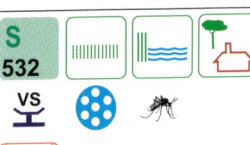

Sand Martin / Europese Oewerswael

Greyish-brown above, white below; white chin, brown breast band, dark underwing coverts, slightly forked tail; mixes with swallow groups

A 533

Brown-throated Martin / Afrikaanse Oewerswael

Mousy-brown above, white below; sometimes completely brown; occurs in flocks usually near water; flight slow and wavering

S 534

In ant bear & porcupine burrows

Banded Martin / Gebande Oewerswael

Sturdy; dark brown above, white below; white line in front of eye, broad brown breast band, white underwing coverts; square tail; slow flyer; scarce

201

Swallow

Small birds with broader wings than swifts; mostly blue backs with forked tails, some showing windows when tail is spread; catch insects in the air.

S 518

Barn Swallow / Europese Swael
Blue-black above, buffy white below; rufous chin and spot on forehead, broad blue-black breast band; forked tail with long outertail feathers

S 520

White-throated Swallow / Witkeelswael
Blue-black above, white below; chestnut forehead, white throat, black breast band; shortish tail with windows; chestnut forehead not visible in young

High rainfall

S 521

Blue Swallow / Blouswael
Completely metallic blue-black; deeply forked tail with very long outertail feathers; purposeful flight close to ground; rare; critically endangered

202

A 522

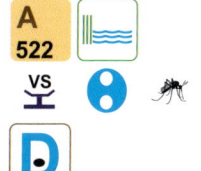

Wire-tailed Swallow / Draadstertswael
Steel-blue above, pure white below with incomplete black vent band; distinct chestnut-reddish crown, outertail feathers resemble two long thin wires, longer in male than in female

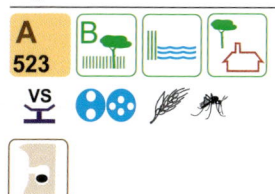

A 523

Pearl-breasted Swallow / Pêrelborsswael
Blue above down to the eye, pure white below; dark rump, black forked tail; unobtrusive; sometimes nests in antbear burrows

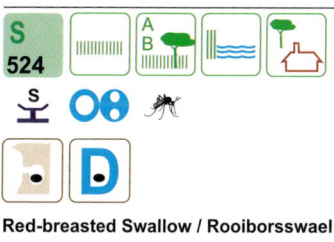

S 524

Red-breasted Swallow / Rooiborsswael
Largest swallow; glossy blue-black above and over ear coverts, rufous below and on rump; tail forked, long outertail feathers; slow gliding flight

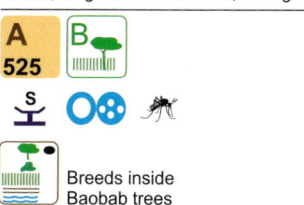

A 525

Breeds inside Baobab trees

Mosque Swallow / Moskeeswael
Glossy blue above, pale rufous below; ear coverts, throat and upper breast whitish, rufous rump, tail deeply forked

Greater Striped Swallow / Grootstreepswael

Blue-black above, white below weakly striped; chestnut cap down to the eye, white ear coverts, pale orange rump, tail with windows; slow gliding flight; calls on the wing

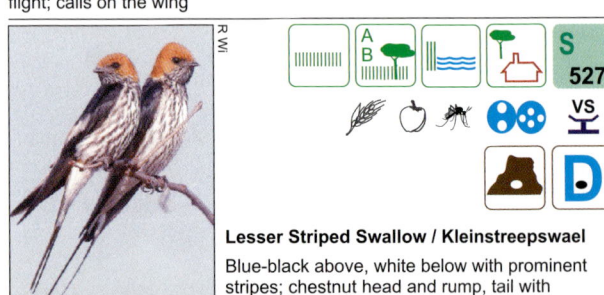

Lesser Striped Swallow / Kleinstreepswael

Blue-black above, white below with prominent stripes; chestnut head and rump, tail with windows; active flight; sometimes in mixed flocks

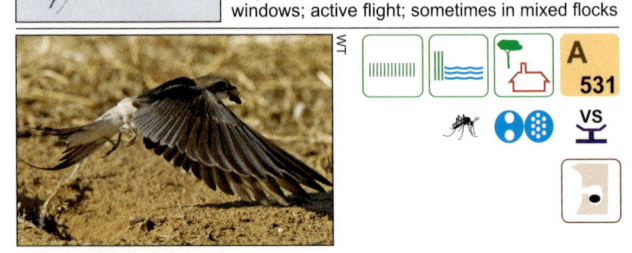

Grey-rumped Swallow / Gryskruisswael

Blue-black above, dull white below washed greyish on breast and flanks; slight eyebrow, greyish crown and rump, deeply forked tail

Black Saw-wing / Swartsaagvlerkswael

Matt black plumage; black underwing coverts, deeply forked tail sharply pointed without streamers; fluttery flight

Swift

Strong and fast flyers; mostly aerial living feeding on insects and even sleeping and pairing on the wing; usually glide; seldom beat their long narrow pointed wings; cannot rise from ground without assistance.

S 411

Common Swift / Europese Windswael

From dark brown to nearly pitch black with deeply forked tail; silent in South Africa

412

African Black Swift / Swartwindswael

Slender; black with whitish chin, contrasting grey-brown secondaries; deeply forked tail; high-pitched call

S 415

Old striped swallow nests

White-rumped Swift / Witkruiswindswael

Dark; whitish on chin and throat, white band on rump; longish deeply forked tail often held closed; high-pitched scream

205

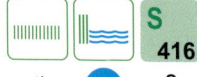

Horus Swift / Horuswindswael

Stocky; black; pale forehead, whitish chin and throat, white rump extending to flanks; broad wings, shallow forked tail

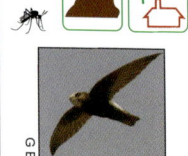

Bee-eater and Banded Martin nests

416

Little Swift / Kleinwindswael

Smallest of swifts; black; white chin, broad white rump; short square tail; twittering call in flight; most common swift

417

Alpine Swift / Witpenswindswael

Largest swift; mouse-brown above, white below; white throat, dark breast band; loud chittering in flight

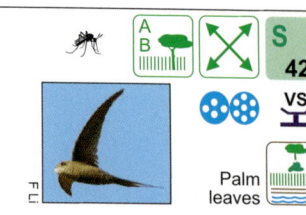

418

African Palm-Swift / Palmwindswael

Slender; mouse-coloured; long pointed wings and tail streamers giving deeply forked effect; twittering call

Palm leaves

421

A 422

Baobab trees

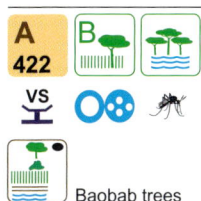

Mottled Spinetail / Gevlekte Stekelstert
Dull dark brown above, dark below with mottled throat and upper breast; very long wings, white rump and vent line, square spined tail; favours areas with Baobab trees

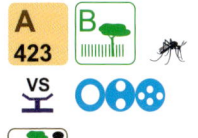

A 423

Baobab trees

Böhm's Spinetail / Witpensstekelstert
Bat-like appearance; sooty black above, whitish below; greyish throat, broad wings, white rump, conspicuous short spined tail; favours areas with Baobab trees

Pratincole

Wide red gapes; short legs, long wings; deeply forked tails. Rest on ground facing into wind. Crepuscular feeder.

S 304

Collared Pratincole / Rooivlerksprinkaanvoël
Dull brown above, whitish below; white eyering, pale yellow throat edged with a thin black line, buff upper breast, dark rufous underwing coverts, white rump

Rare visitors to the Lowveld

7
Black-necked Grebe /
Swartnekdobbertjie

70
Slaty Egret / Rooikeelreier

117
Maccoa Duck /
Bloubekeend

120
Egyptian Vulture /
Egiptiese Aasvoël

147
Palm-nut Vulture /
Witaasvoël

153
Augur Buzzard /
Witborsjakkalsvoël

175
Sooty Falcon /
Roetvalk

177
Eleonora's Falcon /
Eleonoravalk

178
Red-necked Falcon /
Rooinekvalk

186
Pygmy Falcon /
Dwergvalk

208
Blue Crane /
Blou Kraanvoël

Rare visitors to the Lowveld

214
Spotted Crake /
Gevlekte Riethaan

216
Striped Crake /
Gestreepte Riethaan

257
Black-winged Lapwing /
Grootswartvlerkkiewiet

265
Green Sandpiper /
Witgatruiter

279
Pectoral Sandpiper /
Geelpootstrandloper

292
Red-necked
Phalarope /
Rooihalsfraiingpoot

565
Bush Blackcap /
Rooibektiptol

630
Eurasian Reed-Warbler /
Hermanse Rietsanger

692
Collared Flycatcher
in breeding plumage /
Withalsvlieëvanger in
broeikleed

768
Black-bellied
Starling /
Swartpensglansspreeu

786
Variable Sunbird /
Geelpenssuikerbekkie

794
Plain-backed
Sunbird /
Bloukeelsuikerbekkie

209

Rare visitors to the Lowveld

808
Dark-backed Weaver /
Bosmusikant

863
Broad-tailed Paradise-Whydah /
Breëstertparadysvink

909
Wood Pipit /
Boskoester

Vagrants to the Lowveld

109
Northern Pintail /
Pylsterteend

110
Garganey /
Somereend

253
Pacific Golden Plover /
Asiatiese Goue
Strandkiewiet

254
Grey Plover /
Grysstrandkiewiet

268
Common Redshank /
Rooipootruiter

273
Dunlin /
Bontstrandloper

277
White-rumped
Sandpiper /
Witrugstrandloper

278
Baird's Sandpiper /
Bairdse Strandloper

283
Broad-billed Sandpiper /
Breëbekstrandloper

Vagrants to the Lowveld

290
Common Whimbrel /
Kleinwulp

291
Red Phalarope /
Grysfraiingpoot

322
Caspian Tern /
Reusesterretjie

332
Sooty Tern /
Roetsterretjie

379
Barred
Long-tailed Cuckoo /
Langstertkoekoek

434
Mangrove
Kingfisher /
Manglietvisvanger

491 African Pitta /
Angolapitta

610
Boulder Chat /
Swartberglyster

629
Basra
Reed-Warbler /
Basrarietsanger

726
Golden Pipit /
Goudkoester

766
Miombo Blue-eared
Starling /
Kleinblouoorglansspreeu

919
European
Turtle-Dove /
Europese Tortelduif

211

Underwing Patterns

62 Grey Heron /
Bloureier p 33

63 Black-headed Heron /
Swartkopreier p 33

83 White Stork /
Witooievaar p 38

88 Saddle-billed Stork /
Saalbekooievaar p 39

89 Marabou Stork /
Maraboe p 40

91 African Sacred Ibis /
Skoorsteenveër p 40

126 Black Kite /
Swartwou p 83

126.1 Yellow-billed Kite /
Geelbekwou p 83

Underwing Patterns

131 Verreauxs' Eagle / Witkruisarend p 85

139 Long-crested Eagle / Langkuifarend p 87

140 Martial Eagle / Breëkoparend p 85

143 Black-chested Snake-Eagle / Swartborsslangarend p 89

133 Steppe Eagle Juv. / Steppe-arend onvolw. p 86

136 Booted Eagle / Dwergarend p 87

135 Wahlberg's Eagle / Bruinarend p 87

142 Brown Snake-Eagle / Bruinslangarend p 89

Underwing Patterns

146 Bateleur Male /
Berghaan Manlik p 89

146 Bateleur Female /
Berghaan Vroulik p 89

130 European Honey-Buzzard /
Wespedief p 84

141 African Crowned Eagle /
Kroonarend p 86

122 Cape Vulture /
Kransaasvoël p 106

123 White-backed Vulture /
Witrugaasvoël p 106

124 Lappet-faced Vulture /
Swartaasvoël p 107

125 White-headed Vulture /
Witkopaasvoël p 107

Immature Birds

140
Martial Eagle /
Breëkoparend
p 85

161
Gabar Goshawk /
Witkruissperwer
p 94

377
Red-chested
Cuckoo /
Piet-my-vrou
p 184

386
Diderick
Cuckoo /
Diederikkie
p 186

541
Fork-tailed
Drongo /
Mikstertbyvanger
p 179

545
Black-headed
Oriole /
Swartkopwielewaal
p 180

600
Red-capped
Robin-Chat /
Nataljanfrederik
p 163

845
Violet-eared
Waxbill /
Koningblousysie
p 140

215

Immature Birds

146 Bateleur /
Berghaan p 89

380 Great Spotted Cuckoo /
Gevlekte Koekoek p 184

581 Cape Rock-Thrush /
Kaapse Kliplyster p 168

601 Cape Robin-Chat /
Gewone Janfrederik p 164

606 White-starred Robin /
Witkoljanfrederik p 164

732 Common Fiscal /
Fiskaallaksman p 187

834 Green-winged Pytilia /
Gewone Melba p 138

850 Swee Waxbill /
Suidelike Swie p 141

BirdLife SOUTH AFRICA

Founded as the South African Ornithological Society in 1930, their mission is to promote the enjoyment, understanding, conservation and study of birds and their habitat in the wild.

Birdlife runs national and branch programmes and training on conservation, tourism, policy, advocacy, education and awareness. Birdlife South Africa is the partner organisation of Birdlife International, the world's largest voluntary organisation of nationally based conservation organisations, present in more than one hundred countries.

Tel: 011 789 1122, Fax: 011 789 5188
E-mail: info@birdlife.org.za
Website: www.birdlife.org.za

Relevant institutions and websites

African Bird Club (www.africanbirdclub.org)
Birdlife South Africa (www.birdlife.org.za)
Bird Pictures (www.birdpix.nl)
Borrow, Nik (http://web.mac.com/nikborrow)
Clark, Bill (www.raptorresearchfoundation.org)
Eriksen, Hanne & Jens (www.birdsoman.com)
Flickr Photo Sharing (www.flickr.com)
Frost, Willem (www.matlabas.co.za)
Hage, Stefan (www.birds.se)
Horton, Tom (http://furthertofly.imagekind.com)
Nagtegaal, Rob (http://www.pbase.com/tonbenrob)
Oiseaux (www.oiseaux.net)
Oscarsson, Stefan (www.osqar.se)
Photographer's Base (www.pbase.com)
RSA Bird Spotter's Guides (www.adverta.co.za)
SOS/BirdLife Slovensko (www.vtaky.sk)
Sylvan Heights Waterfowl Park (www.sylvanheights.org)
Van den Broeck, J (www.migrantbird.com)
Vang Kevin (www.birdquest.net)

Glossary

aquatic	- living in or on water
beak	- strong hooked bill, eg. birds of prey
bill	- beak, especially when slender
bobbing	- up and down movement
bristles	- short stiff hairs
call	- used in alarm or for contact
carpal	- wrist, shoulder of wing
carpal spur	- thornlike protrusion on wing shoulder
casque	- extra growth on top of the bill
cere	- waxy membrane at base of the beak
colonial	- where nests are clumped together
conical	- shaped like a cone
coverts	- protective feathers covering others
crepuscular	- active at dusk or dawn
crest	- elongated feathers on head
cryptic	- colours blend into surroundings
diurnal	- active during the day
ear tufts	- bunch of feathers resembling ears
flock	- large number of birds together
frontal shield	- bare growth on forehead
gape	- corner of bill or beak
gregarious	- living in flocks or communities
head-dip	- head submerged, tail-end protruding
hover	- hanging in air rapidly beating wings
juvenile	- young or immature bird
lore	- fleshy area between bill and eye
mandible	- bill or beak
melanistic	- excessive black pigmentation
morph	- alternative permanent colour form
nocturnal	- night active
nomadic	- roaming from area to area
parasitic	- non-breeding; lays eggs in host's nest
pectoral patch	- feather cluster on side of breast
primaries	- outermost major flight feathers
polyandrous	- female mates with more than one male
polygynous	- male mates with more than one female
raptor	- carnivorous bird of prey
song	- melodious series of notes
speculum	- patch of coloured feathers on the wing
talons	- sharply hooked claws
trill	- sound by vibration of tongue
vent area	- undertail region
vermiculated	- marked with narrow wavy lines
wattle	- bare fleshy appendage
web	- skin between toes
window	- patch with window-like appearance

Acknowledgements

Amyras, J (J Am), Atkinson, Grant (G At), Attard, Billy (B At), Azafzaf, Hichem (H Az), Bakker, Kees (K Ba), Barnes, Dave (DB), Bastaja, Daniel (D Ba), Bianchi, Sergio (S Bi), Bisschop, Herman (H Bi), Böhmer, Rudy (R Bo), Borrow, Nik (N Bo), Bosman, Annette (A Bo), Botha, André (A Bot), Brickell, Neville (N Br), Brown, Susan (S Br), Buckton, Cliff (C Bu), Butler, Neil (N Bu), Chudý, Andrej (AC), Cox, Brian (B Co), Czupryna, Stephen (St Cz), Dansen, Koos (K Da), Dawe, Justin (J Da), De Bruyn, Jody (JdB), Dedicoat, Peter (P De), De Voogt, Willem (WdV), De Wet, Callie (CdW), Dikkers, Henk (H Di), Dikkers, Willie (W Di), Dreyer, Francois (F Dr), Du Preez, Johann (JdP), Du Toit, André (AdT), Eckström, Göran (G Ec), Engelbrecht, D (D En), Enslin, Piet (PE), Erard, Jacques (J Er), Eriksen, Hanne & Jens (H J Er), Faustino, Augusto (A Fa), Fikkert, Cor (C Fi), Fischer, Mark (Ma F), Foley, Con (CF), Forsman, Dick (D Fo), Fourie, Philip (Ph Fo), Francia, Marlene (M Fr), Franke, Ursula (U Fr), Frost, Willem (W Fr), Fry, Philip (PF), Furniss, Graham (G Fu), Garvie, Steve & Ngala, David (St Ga), Germain, Luc (L Ger), Giannotti, Agnes (A Gi), Ginn, Peter (PG), GNU (GNU), Goetz, André (A Go), Goetz, Martin (M Go), Goodey, Martin (Ma Go), Gray, Neil (N Gr), Greyling, Tischa (T Gr), Grieve, Graham (GG), Grosel, Joe (J Gr), Gutteridge, Lee (L G), Haagner, Clem (CH), Hall, Elaine (E Ha), Hall, Ken (K Ha), Hamilton, John (JH), Hanegraaf, Lee (LH), Hardaker, Andrew (A Ha), Hardaker, Trevor (Tr Ha), Harmse, Ben (BH), Harris, T (T Ha), Hazell, Gareth (G Ha), Helsens, Thiery (T He), Hesper, Tineke (Ti He), Heymans, Joseph (J He), Hill, R (R Hi), Hofmann, Gerhard (G Hof), Holtshausen, Gordon (G Ho), Hopkins, Adrian (A Hop), Horton, Tom (T Ho), Hut, Eddy (E Hu), Janse van Rensburg, J (JJvR), Janse van Rensburg, Sammy (SJvR), Kahn, Rudi (R Ka), Kakebeeke, Ben (B Ka), Kalwij, Joeri (J Ka), Kampf, Ruud (R Ka), Kaplan, Clive (CK), Kelly, Mike (M Ke), Kelson, Doug (D Ke), Kemp, Alan (A Ke), Kennedy, Adam Scott (AK), Kennekam, Myburgh (Mybs), Kidson, Saartjie (S Ki), Kolbeinsson, Yann (YK), Koskinen, Juha (J Ko), Kristiansen, Ernst (E Kr), Krog, Ole (O Kr), Langelaan, Marcel (M La), Lasley, Greg (Gr La), Lewis, Bob (B Le), Libert, Francois (F Li), Manson, Alan (A Ma), Marais, PBW 'Dienkie' APSSA (D Ma), Maree, Christine (C Ma), Massie, David (D Mas), MacKay, Stuart (SM), Montinaro, Richard (R Mo), Morris, Pete (PM), Moul, Bob (B Mo), NASA (NA), Nagtegaal, Rob (R Na), Nason, Ian (I Na), Newell, Dick (Di N), Noakes, Paul (P No), Odekerken, P (P Od), Olioso, Georges (G Oli), Oscarsson, Stefan (SO), Otten, Rico (R Ot), Patel, Shailesh (S Pa), Paxton, Mark (M Pa), Peeters, Hans (H Pe), Pen, Andries (AP), Penlington, Phil (P Pe), Perkins, Megan (M Pe), Pienaar, Kobus (KP), Plowes, Darell (D Pl), Raijmakers, Kobie (KR), Ravno, Kevin (Ke Ra), Reinecke, Eddie (ER), Roberts, Victor (V Ro), Selch, Ulla & Kim (U K Se), Semler, Dave (DS), Shani, Itai (I Sh), Siyawareva, Benson (B Si), Skov, Soren (S Sk), Smitterberg, Per (PS), Snyders, Leon (L Sn), Sperka, Christian (C Sp), Spies, Hein (HS), Steenekamp, Nic (N St), Stobbs, Simon (Si St), Sussens, Q (QS), Swanepoel, Dewald (D Sw), Swanepoel, Frans (F Sw), Tarboton, Warwick (WT), Tarrant, Tom (TT), Tenovuo, Jorma (J Te), Theron, Gerhard (G Th), Thompson, Fiona (F Th), Todd, Frank S. (F To), Toupin, Yvon (Y To), Transvaal Museum (TM), Trochain, Celine (CT), Uys, Wynand (W Uys), Van Bosch, Michael (MvB), Van den Broek, Ben (BvdB), Van den Broeck, Jan (JvdB), Van der Greef, J (JvdG), Vang, Kevin (KV), Van Niekerk, Herman (HvN), Van Reenen, Archie, Van Rensburg, Martin (MvR), Van Schalkwyk, Peet (PvS), Van Zalinge, Nic (NvZ), Van Zalinge, Robert (RvZ), Van Zoest, Peter (PvZ), Veen, Brenda (Br Ve), Veldman, Mich (MV), Veldt, Michel (Mi Ve), Viana, José (J Vi), Vlot Ruben & Jorrit (R&J Vlot), Wagner, Rudolf (Ru Wa), Waschkies, Reinhild (R Wa), Weber, F (F We), Weiss, James (JW), Wienand, Robert (R Wi), Wilson, Ray (Ray W), Wursten, Bart (BW), Yates, Mark (M Ya), Shapefinder: BH, TM JAm, MV, YK, A Fa, N Gr.

Bibliography

Publications
Birds of Prey – Pickford & Tarboton
Identifying Warblers in the Hand – Raijmakers & Raijmakers
Kingfishers, Bee-Eaters and Rollers – Fry, Fry & Harris
Kingfishers of Sub-Saharan Africa – Clancy
LBJ's Made Easier – Newman, Solomon, Johnson & Masterson
Nests and Eggs of Southern African Birds – Tarboton
Newman se Voëls van Suider-Afrika – Newman
Owls and Owling – Tarboton & Erasmus
Roberts Birds of Southern Africa – Gordon Maclean, 6th Edition
Roberts Birds of Southern Africa – Hockey, Dean & Ryan, 7th Edition
Roofvoëls – Oberprieler & Cillié
Sakgids tot Suider-Afrikaanse Voëls – Cillié & Oberprieler
South African Birds – Gill
Spotter's Guide to Birds of the Bushveld – Kidson & Van Niekerk
Suider-Afrikaanse Voëls – Sinclair & Davidson
The Atlas of Southern African Birds Vol 1 & 2 – Harrison, Allen, Underhill, Herremans, Tree, Parker & Brown (ADU)
The Birds Around Us – Liversidge & Adams
The Official Checklist of Birds in Southern Africa – BirdLife South Africa
The RSPB Book of British Birds – Holde, Sharrock & Burn
Veldgids – Voëls van Suider-Afrika – Prozesky
Voëls van Suider-Afrika – Sinclair, Hockey & Tarboton
Waders of Southern Africa – Hockey & Douie

Journals, papers etc.
'n Gids tot die Lewerikke van Suider-Afrika – Oberprieler
Pipits of Southern Africa – Peacock
Birds and Birding
Laniarius
Bokmakierie

100 p. 16

861 p. 131

About the authors

Saartjie Kidson

Obtained a diploma in Clinical Pathology at the Witwatersrand Technical College.

After many years devoted to orchid growing and national and international judging she is now a retired Orchid Judge.

Has lived at the foot of the Waterberg in the glorious Bushveld since 1999.

She is a fanatical bird watcher and Founder of the Naboomspruit Bird Club, and qualified specialist tour guide. She is a frequent visitor to the Lowveld.

She is also an avid outdoor person. Hobbies include travelling to far places for the rare and elusive birds of the world, reading, writing, indulging in poetry, gardening and studying trees and butterflies.

Herman van Niekerk

Studied at the University of Pretoria and holds, amongst various others, the qualifications BA Hons CEA.

Involved in wildlife and nature conservation, environmental matters, archaeology and tourism since 1969. Member of the Wildlife Environmental Society of South Africa for more than 30 years.

Founder member of the Friends of Nylsvley in 1987, and qualified specialist tour guide

Former owner and editor of *Aves* bird magazine and *Natura* nature magazine. Author of 11 books and more than 300 articles, short stories and essays as well as poetry in English and Afrikaans.

Hobbies include art and photography. Some of the photographs in this series of bird guides are from his collection.

Donated comprehensive collection of South African butterflies to Transvaal Museum for educational purposes.

Hails from a family of Lowveld pioneers. Resides in the Bushveld.

Notes

Notes

Spotter's Guide to Birds of the Lowveld also on DVD

The Spotter's Guide to the Birds of the Lowveld is also available on an interactive DVD for computer. The 541 resident bird species of the Lowveld are included on the DVD, while the calls of most of them have been added and can be heard with the click of a button next to each photograph. Information can be viewed on the web page www.adverta.co.za

The DVD is obtainable from the authors at e-mail address info@adverta.co.za.

CD of Southern African Bird Calls

The bilingual CD Wild Bird Calls of Southern Africa, with the calls of 208 of South Africa's most well-known birds, and those with pleasant songs, is obtainable from the compilers, S. C. Kidson en H. L. Van Niekerk. The CD includes a complete bilingual reference list to assist with easy navigation between the different bird calls on the CD. The authors can be contacted by e-mail at info@adverta.co.za

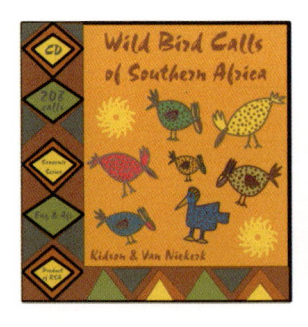

Key

- 🔴 Cities and towns
- 🟢 Game and nature reserves

Climate	Subtropical to tropical
Temperature	Hot summers, warm winters. 6° to 42° C, average 23° C. Warm evenings, average 19° C.
Rainfall	620 mm in the east dwindling to 350 mm in the west.
Vegetation	In the east predominantly sweet Lowveld bushveld with abundant broad-leaved trees and some indigenous forests along the escarpment. Drier more sour bushveld and mopaniveld with baobab trees to the north and west